Perfect Slow Cooking

Other titles in the *Perfect* series

Perfect
Slow Cooking

Elizabeth Brown

BOOKS

Published by Random House Books 2010
1 2 3 4 5 6 7 8 9 10

Copyright © Grapevine Publishing Services 2010

Elizabeth Brown has asserted her right under the Copyright, Designs
and Patents Act, 1988, to be identified as the author of this work

First published in Great Britain in 2010 by
Random House Books
Random House, 20 Vauxhall Bridge Road,
London SW1V 2SA

www.rbooks.co.uk

Addresses for companies within The Random House Group Limited
can be found at: www.randomhouse.co.uk/offices.htm

The Random House Group Limited Reg. No. 954009

A CIP catalogue record for this book
is available from the British Library

ISBN 9781847946058

The Random House Group Limited makes every effort to ensure that
the papers used in its books are made from trees that have been legally
sourced from well-managed and credibly certified forests. Our paper
procurement policy can be found at
www.randomhouse.co.uk/paper.htm

Typeset by Delineate for Grapevine Publishing Services Ltd

Printed and bound in Great Britain by
CPI Bookmarque, Croydon, CR0 4TD

Contents

Meat

1 Getting Started

Slow cooking couldn't be easier, and, unlike many other methods of cooking, you need little equipment and just a handful of tips to bear in mind as you go. Once you've mastered the basics, you'll be able to adapt almost any recipe for your slow cooker.

Why slow cook?

Today's busy lifestyle offers little time to prepare and cook fresh, wholesome meals, yet we are all increasingly aware of the need to eat well and to obtain the maximum nutritional benefit from our food. Furthermore, with the cost of food rising and our budgets becoming ever tighter, most of us need to adjust the way we shop and cook to get better value for money.

That's where slow cooking comes in. Not only will you spend the least possible time preparing meals – popping your ingredients straight into the slow cooker where they can be cooked throughout the day while you get on with other things – but you can choose cheaper ingredients too. For example, pulses, root vegetables, frozen produce and the tougher cuts of meat lend themselves beautifully to slow cooking.

Slow cooking is also a healthy way to prepare food. Most of the foods you will be cooking will simmer away in their own juices, preserving the vitamins and minerals they contain in the sauces you create. Unlike many cooking methods in which you discard the cooking water along with the nutrients, you'll be using your slow-cooking liquids to enhance the taste and flavour of your meals.

Slow cookers are inexpensive to operate, requiring only a little electricity, and for the same reason, they are an environmentally friendly alternative to oven or stove-top cooking. In fact, the average slow cooker uses about the same amount of electricity as a lightbulb. Savings vary between models, and according to what you are cooking, but you can rest assured that making your meals in a slow cooker will save you money and help you to do your bit for the planet too.

Slow cookers are also ideal for hot weather, as they generate very little heat, keeping your kitchen – and you – cool. What's more, you won't be slaving over a hot stove all day.

Apart from a little chopping and perhaps some browning or marinating, the preparation is very simple, after which your creations take care of themselves.

Timing isn't an issue, either. If you're not ready when your meal is, you can simply turn the slow cooker to low and keep it warm until the time is right to eat. The quality of the food you have prepared will not be affected to any significant degree, no matter how long you keep it cooking. So if you are a busy parent and need to get food on the table at lunchtime, you can use the slow cooker on a higher setting, then turn it down to keep the food warm and tasty for later. Similarly, if you need to get hot food on the table for the children earlier, then turn down the setting to keep it warm for a second sitting for adults later. You'll always have a healthy meal to hand, without the need for reheating, which can change the flavour and consistency of many dishes.

Slow cookers are traditionally associated with heavy stews, soups and casseroles; however, it's perfectly possible to create lighter alternatives, including fresh fish dishes, summery puddings, seasonal vegetable dishes, and jams or condiments. You can even pre-cook the makings of a fantastic barbecue, popping it on to the grill once it's cooked, for that distinctive flavour and crispiness. Slow cookers are also ideal for dishes that are eaten cold; after cooking, simply refrigerate dishes such as pâtés, soups, cold meats or fish, fresh desserts and compôtes.

There is even something for real food connoisseurs. You can create a multitude of sauces and jus, seasoned with herbs, spices, fruit and their juices, wine and cider, and just about anything else – all with minimal effort. Flavours that are cooked together over longer periods of time have the opportunity to blend and develop, and everything becomes mouth-wateringly tender. You can also use the slow cooker to keep foods that you have prepared in the oven, or on the hob, fresh and warm before serving.

Whether you are on your own and want to create tasty meals with the minimum of fuss, a student with limited cooking facilities, out at work all day with little time to prepare healthy meals, a busy mum or dad with your hands full or if you're just looking for quicker, easier ways to create gourmet meals, slow cooking is for you.

Buying a slow cooker

Thanks to the growing demand for quick and easy methods of cooking, as well as concern about the environment and the household budget, slow cooking has become increasingly popular, and there is now a wide range of slow cookers on the market. Although the cheaper brands may be appealing, and work perfectly well, you might want to consider everything that's available, as some models have added features that will help you to expand your slow-cooking repertoire.

First, you will need to consider the amount of space you have. A slow cooker that is in constant use should ideally have its own place on the kitchen worktop, rather than being lifted in and out of a cupboard. Slow cookers come in all shapes and sizes, so you might find that a slimmer oval cooker, for example, fits your space requirements better.

The capacity is also important. These days, you can get slow cookers that will hold anything from 1½ to about 4 litres (around 2½–7 pints). If you are cooking regularly for guests or a family, it's always worth going for the larger models. Slow cookers do, however, tend to operate most efficiently when they are at least half full – smaller quantities can sometimes cook too quickly or even burn. So, if you regularly cook single portions, go for a smaller model. The cooking pots inside a slow cooker are normally earthenware, which provides excellent insulation and conducts the heat evenly. You can also find models with aluminium pots, which can be used directly on the hob for browning or caramelising ingredients prior to cooking in the pot. There are drawbacks with these, however. Some research has suggested that ingesting high levels of aluminium can lead to Alzheimer's disease and that it can be absorbed from pots into food. Secondly, acidic foods, such as tomatoes, lemons, cabbage, rhubarb and many soft fruits, can react with the metal, which alters their taste significantly.

You can also purchase 'fixed-pot' cookers, which do not have a removable pot or lining. These tend to be extremely energy efficient, but can be difficult to clean, as they cannot be immersed in water because of the built-in electrical connections. You'll also need to decant the contents into a separate serving dish, whereas the removable pots can be used for serving as well as cooking.

Different-sized slow cookers are good for different dishes. For example, puddings, stews, casseroles, soups and condiments tend to work best in deeper pots, while fish, individual puddings, stuffed peppers, drier foods (like ribs or even burgers) and whole roasts do better in more shallow, oval models. Depending upon how much you use the slow cooker, you may even want to invest in both!

Lids can be glass, stainless steel, plastic, aluminium or earthenware, and should fit firmly over the pot to ensure that steam and/or heat do not escape. However, they should be capable of being moved slightly from side to side, while not rocking on the base. Some people prefer glass lids, not only because they allow you to see the contents while cooking, but also because they tend to be more robust. Lids with a high dome are ideal, because they allow more room for cooking 'taller' foods, such as chickens and whole roasts; they also help to prevent a slightly overfilled cooker from expelling its contents all over the kitchen work surface!

The base of the slow cooker should be sturdy, with good, solid handles. When full, slow cookers can be very heavy, and you'll need to make sure that the model you choose can withstand plenty of lifting. Avoid models with plastic handles and/or metal rims, which tend to be difficult to keep clean (with food building up along the seams) and less durable. There must be space for the air to flow under the unit, and it should also be kept away from the wall or other appliances while cooking, to allow any heat to dissipate.

The more heat settings, the better. Low settings tend to be used for dishes that will be cooked throughout the day (or night), and will heat and cook the food slowly. High settings are used for meals that need to be on the table more quickly or to speed up cooking. You'll also use high settings for cooking things like roasts, cakes and steamed puddings, which need to reach a high temperature fairly quickly, or to boost the temperature, if it's all taking too long. Automatic settings are very important, so make sure you choose a model that has this feature. When set to automatic, slow cookers will normally begin cooking on high, then, when the temperature reaches a certain point, automatically reduce the heat for the remainder of the cooking period. Furthermore, once cooking is complete, a good slow cooker will automatically switch to 'keep warm', to prevent overcooking. This is an essential feature if you are unlikely to be around when cooking is finished.

Having said that, there is nothing wrong with models that have three basic settings: low, high and warm. As long as someone is around to turn the machine down or off at the end of cooking time, there shouldn't be any problems.

If possible, choose a model with a timer. This will allow you to set the slow cooker to begin its work while you are out (or when you go to sleep) and to stop when it's finished. So, for example, if you're preparing a stew that takes six hours to cook, and you are going to be out of the house for eight hours, you can set the timer to begin two hours after you leave. This works beautifully for many dishes, although you must be careful to ensure that your food is well chilled before being placed in the pot, as leaving it sitting around for long periods before cooking begins can encourage the growth of bacteria (see page 27).

It probably goes without saying that the more features, the higher the cost, so if you have a tight budget, go for a model that is simple to operate. Finally, one thing that is a must, but is not included in every model, is an indicator light. It may sound ridiculous, but you do need to know that the slow cooker is actually on and working. They can take some time to heat up and, because they release very little heat, you may not realise that your supper isn't cooking until you open the pot to raw food.

Using your slow cooker

Slow cooking couldn't be simpler, but there are a few tips to bear in mind to ensure success every time. First, make sure you always set the temperature correctly. Cooking your pot roast on high for a day will not result in a tender, moist meal. Every recipe in this book has a suggested temperature to ensure the best results, and it's important that you use it. In general, the low setting is designed to be about 95°C (200°F), while the high setting normally reaches about 150°C (300°F). These temperatures are adequate to destroy bacteria and to ensure even cooking, while retaining moisture and flavour in the dish.

If you are in a rush, you may wish to cook things at a higher temperature. If this is the case, you should be aware that the cooking time on 'high' is just over half of that on 'low'.

Slow cookers operate differently according to the model, and you may need to experiment a little to get the results you want. Check cooking times in the manufacturer's instruction booklet, and if they differ wildly from what I suggest here, then go with what they recommend or somewhere in between. For the first few recipes, check your food towards the end of cooking to see how it's getting on. It's a good idea to allow a little extra time, just in case.

In almost every case, the slow cooker should be preheated before use. This helps to ensure that the heat is evenly distributed and also that no bacteria build up in the ingredients during the 'warming-up' process. It's particularly important to preheat if you are roasting a joint or a chicken, as it needs to reach a high temperature as quickly as possible.

Cut vegetables and meat into smallish chunks for better cooking. If you are using whole vegetables or joints, make sure you allow enough time for them to cook thoroughly.

Many recipes require you to brown some elements of the dish before decanting into the slow cooker. This helps to improve the flavour and the appearance of the food – particularly meat. It's worth noting, however, that it's not an essential step and if you are pressed for time, you may not mind putting up with pale-skinned chicken or slightly grey meat.

For a thicker sauce or soup, you can toss your ingredients in flour before browning. This will combine with any natural or added fats in the dish to thicken the juices, and it will also 'seal' the meat to ensure it remains as tender as possible.

If you are cooking with liquid (as in the case of stews or soups), these should, ideally, be added to the slow cooker hot. So boil the kettle while the slow cooker warms up. A simple stock cube in boiling water or some orange juice heated in the microwave will make a delicious base for many recipes.

When loading the slow cooker, in general make sure that root vegetables, such as onions, carrots and other 'sturdier' fare, are placed in the bottom of the cooker first. Then add the meat and other ingredients. Cover with herbs and seasoning, then pour over enough hot cooking liquid to cover the food, but not engulf it (the vegetables should be immersed). Remember that most foods produce their own liquid while cooking, so the level will rise as cooking proceeds. You'll soon get the hang of how to load the slow cooker according to the foods you are cooking.

In some cases, you'll need to add other foods later. For example, green beans or broccoli work well when they are 'steamed' on top of whatever else is cooking. You'll need to add these quickly though, and all in one go, because lifting the lid of your cooker will break the water seal, thus releasing the heat. Ideally, they should be room temperature, rather than frozen (see page 23).

Don't be tempted to lift the lid to check on your cooking. The heat loss will extend your cooking time significantly, particularly if you check it in the early stages of cooking, when the slow cooker is working towards establishing optimal heat. Every time you lift the lid, you can expect to add about 20 to 30 minutes to your cooking time. It isn't usually necessary to stir the contents of the slow cooker, although this can vary between recipes. You can safely lift the lid towards the end of the cooking period, but remember that it will add a few more minutes to the overall cooking time.

Make sure the slow cooker is positioned on a sturdy surface. You may wish to place it on a tea towel, which will absorb any liquid that spits or spills out. Although the steam produces a seal that keeps the heat and the contents in the pot, hot liquid may sometimes escape when the pressure builds up. This won't affect the contents, but can damage surfaces.

When cooking is complete, the slow cooker may automatically switch to 'warm', or you can manually reduce the heat to the lowest setting. It will stay warm and fresh for several hours. If you have leftovers, remove them from the pot, transfer them to a clean container, let them cool slightly and then refrigerate or freeze. Don't allow food to cool in the slow cooker itself, as it retains its heat for a long time and bacteria can build up during the cooling process.

In Part Two (see pages 30–149), we'll look at tips for cooking various types of food; however, it's worth mentioning the following now:

- Most liquids can be used in a slow cooker, but remember that you'll need less liquid than you would for traditionally cooked meals. The reason for this is that there is almost no evaporation, and the contents of the slow cooker will also release their own moisture.
- Pasta and rice can be cooked in a slow cooker (contrary to what many manufacturers suggest). However, they should be added in the last 30 to 40 minutes of cooking time, to ensure that they don't become soggy. If you are using lasagne or cannelloni, choose fresh brands, or immerse dried sheets in some boiling water before using to ensure even cooking. All of the pasta should be covered with sauce throughout cooking, or it will become hard and dry.
- Easy-cook rice is probably your best bet, but if you are using a speciality rice for particular dishes (as in the case of risotto, for example), you will need to break the golden rule and open your pot for stirring. This helps to ensure that the water is absorbed evenly, and that the rice is well cooked. If you are adding rice to stews or soups, do so in the final 30 minutes of cooking time.
- Both pasta and rice absorb liquid, so you will need to add an extra 150ml (5fl oz) of fluid for every 50g (1¾oz) of pasta or rice.
- Dried pulses can be cooked beautifully in a slow cooker, but they should always be soaked overnight before being added (apart from

lentils, which can be added in dry form). Red kidney beans should
be boiled for ten minutes before being added to destroy the natural
toxins they contain. Tinned pulses simply need to be drained.

- Some recipes have toppings that require a quick browning under
the grill, or a period of baking. In most cases, you can transfer the
slow cooker's removable pot to do this.

- Because the liquid content of a slow cooker increases with cooking,
you may need to thicken any sauces by continuing to cook for a
period of time without the lid on the pot, or begin cooking with a
sauce that is thicker than usual. For example, if you are cooking
fish in a white wine sauce, add extra cornflour or make the roux
thicker before adding it to the pot.

Faster cooking in a slow cooker

Slow cookers aren't just for slow cooking! There is a variety of ways in
which you can speed up the process and cook all elements of your meal
in a single pot:

- To begin with, browning or softening ingredients such as meat and
onions can help to speed up the process. They'll need considerably
less time in the slow cooker if they are already on their way to
being cooked.

- Many recipes require you to preheat the slow cooker. If it's hot and
ready to go, you'll cut your cooking time by an hour or so.

- Make sure you add hot liquid to the slow cooker; even if you are
using fruit juice or wine, it's worth giving it a zap in the microwave
before adding it to your pot.

- Leave your cooker on high for longer at the beginning of the cooking time. In some cases, you can cook your entire meal on high,
and it will be ready several hours earlier.

- Remember, keep your hands off the lid – every time you lift the
top of a slow cooker you'll release the heat and break the seal, and
it will take at least 20 minutes to regain its cooking temperature.

- Experiment with the slow cooker. Some cook food faster than others, and some have more sensitive controls allowing you to choose the temperature rather than relying on more general 'high' or 'low' settings. It's a good idea to try out a recipe or two over the weekend, when you are home to check progress.
- Finish off in the oven or on the hob. If you manage to get everything just about there while you are out and about, it's a simple process to return home and give the contents a blast in the oven to speed things up. Earthenware pots are oven safe, so you can transfer them across without decanting the contents.
- Remember that one hour of cooking on the high setting is roughly equal to two and a half hours of cooking on low. Many recipes can be adapted for faster cooking, although roasts and cheaper cuts of meat usually benefit from longer cooking times. Baking must also be undertaken at the suggested temperature, as the more delicate mechanisms involved in making it a success are temperature sensitive.
- Once you've 'fast cooked' in the slow cooker, you can turn down the temperature and keep it warm for later on.

Essential equipment

One of the most appealing features of a slow cooker is the fact that very little equipment is required. The idea is that you can throw all of your ingredients into a pot, then forget about them until dinner is served. There are, however, a few essential items that can make slow cooking easier than ever, and help you to expand your slow-cooking repertoire.

- A heavy-bottomed, non-stick frying pan – for browning meat and softening vegetables, such as onions and leeks. Choose one with deep sides to contain larger cuts of meat. Non-stick isn't essential, but it means you can use less fat when preparing your food.
- A slotted spoon – to remove vegetables and meat from a frying pan to the slow cooker, and from the slow cooker to the plate.

- A small springform pan – for cakes and other desserts. Choose one that sits flat in the base of the slow cooker, with a little space around the outside so you can grip the pan for removal.
- A large pudding basin or soufflé dish – for puddings, cakes and other desserts. It should fit inside the slow cooker without raising the lid. You may also choose individual basins and dishes which can be seated side by side along the base of the cooker.
- A wire rack – to sit in the bottom of the slow cooker and elevate foods or dishes you do not want to cook in liquid.
- A lifting strap – to lift tight-fitting basins, pans and dishes from the slow cooker. You can either purchase a silicone lifting strap, or fashion one from a wide strip of thin, rubberised tablecloth fabric. The idea is that you simply place it under your dish or pan and lift it into the slow cooker; then replace the lid and cook with the ends of the strap hanging out. Press down hard on the lid to ensure that you create a seal. When cooking is complete, remove the lid and use the strap to lift out your cooked meal.
- A hand blender or food processor – ideal for creating delicious soups or smooth sauces from the cooking liquids. You could also whiz up vegetable purées and fruit coulis to serve on the side.
- A good set of oven gloves or pot-holders – slow cookers get hot during the cooking process and you will need protection.

Some recipes will require a little extra equipment, and you'll find details of anything you'll need at the beginning of each recipe in this book. But rest assured, slow cooking is remarkably easy, and you'll find you already have most of what you need just waiting for an airing!

Seasoning and flavour

You can use any type of seasoning to provide your slow-cooked dishes with a multitude of different flavours. There are a few things to bear in mind, as the slow-cooking process can intensify some flavours, while robbing it from other ingredients:

- Choose dried herbs over fresh, whenever possible. Fresh herbs will go brown and limp in the long, moist cooking process, eventually becoming flavourless. Whole dried herbs and spices will release their flavour over time, and are better that ground herbs for slow cooking. If you do choose to use fresh herbs, wait until the last 30 minutes of cooking before adding them.
- The flavour of some herbs and spices intensifies while cooking, and you'll need to use a little less than you would when cooking the traditional way. These include bay leaves, lime leaves, ginger, thyme and rosemary. 'Lighter' herbs, such as parsley, marjoram, basil, coriander, dill and tarragon may need to be added in larger quantities.
- Dried herbs and spices should be added at the beginning of cooking. However, some varieties, such as chilli, ginger and mustard seeds, can become bitter if cooked for too long, and should only be added about halfway through the cooking process. A number of Indian spices fall into this category, and should be added later on. If you are planning to be out and won't have access to the slow cooker, they can be added near the end of the cooking time with good results.
- Whole spices, such as peppercorns, cinnamon sticks, coriander seeds, cumin seeds and aniseed, are better suited to slow cooking as they release their flavour slowly.
- Condiments can be used to flavour your slow-cooked meals, including curry pastes, soy, hoisin, Worcestershire, fish and oyster sauces and ketchup. A little goes a long way, so add less than you would to season traditionally cooked dishes, and taste for flavour during the cooking process. Remember that strong, spicy flavours are enhanced through slow cooking.
- Adding alcohol is an excellent way to add flavour to your dishes, but go gently! When you use alcohol in traditionally prepared dishes, most of the alcohol evaporates, leaving just the flavour. However, because less liquid evaporates when you slow cook, the alcohol will retain more of its alcohol content (something to consider if you are serving your whole family). Aim to use about half

the amount you would normally. Beer, cider and wine are all good options, as are spirits, such as rum, which can be used to flavour desserts.

- Extracts of vanilla, peppermint or almond, as well as lighter 'waters', such as rose or orange flower water, can enhance the flavour of both savoury and sweet dishes. Be sure to add only a few drops of each, as the flavours grow and develop when they are cooked. Lighter waters should be added towards the end of cooking to ensure that they don't lose their flavour.

- Garlic and onions can be added as usual, as the flavours mellow and mingle when they are slow cooked, without dominating or tasting bitter. Whole garlic cloves and big chunks of onion can be used, as there is plenty of time for them to impart their flavour.

- Try not to skip the browning process. When you brown meats and vegetables, you caramelise the sugars on their surfaces, developing their flavours substantially. What's more, the browned bits remaining at the bottom of the pan, which can be scraped into the slow cooker, are known as *fond* in French, because they provide the foundation for the flavour of the entire dish.

- Liquid doesn't escape in the slow cooker, which means that recipes intended for the hob or oven may become watery. Liquid usually needs to be reduced by 50 per cent after cooking, but you can achieve this by leaving the top off the cooker and turning the heat up to high for about 30 minutes. You can add fresh herbs and other seasonings at this stage, as well as some alcohol, and use thickeners such as potato, corn or wheat flour.

Adapting recipes for a slow cooker

Many recipes can be adapted for slow cooking, but it can be a trial-and-error process. To begin with, see if you can find a recipe in this book that's similar to the one you're interested in, just to give you an idea of cooking times and the order in which to load the ingredients into the slow cooker. This will also help you to work out how much flavouring you'll need. The following tips will help you to make your recipe a success:

- Anything that is simmered, braised, stewed or slow roasted will work well in a slow cooker, but think beyond obvious candidates; risottos and desserts, for example, are easy to make in a slow cooker.
- Browning meats (dredged first in flour with herbs or spices) can make your final dish look more appealing and enhance the taste.
- Go easy on the liquids, as foods yield liquid during the cooking process and using too much will dilute the taste. Most recipes require about half as much liquid when prepared in a slow cooker. If the original recipe includes liquid that is lost during cooking (through evaporation, for example), reduce this accordingly when slow cooking.
- Conversely, remember that at least some moisture is required for slow cooking. So if the original recipe is entirely dry, you may have to add some liquid. See the recipes in part two for examples of how different foods are cooked.
- No matter which herbs or spices you are using, taste for seasoning about 30 minutes to an hour before serving and adjust as required. Remember, fresh herbs should only be added at this stage.
- Fresh milk, cheese, sour cream, crème fraîche, yoghurt and other dairy products can break down during slow cooking and separate. Add them in the last hour of cooking or make sure they are stabilised – in a roux or white sauce, for example. Evaporated milk can be used for the whole of the cooking process.
- Defrost frozen vegetables and add them, along with anything 'green', such as broccoli or green beans, in the last 15 to 45 minutes, depending upon the temperature.
- If you are cooking a recipe with rice, add an extra 75ml (3fl oz) of water for every 50g (1¾oz) of rice.
- Fish and shellfish can disintegrate easily if they are cooked for long periods of time, so stir them in about an hour before the end of cooking time. There are some other ways to cook fish and shellfish that don't require you to be standing by the pot (see page 89).

- Generally speaking, 1–2kg (2¼–4½lb) of boneless meat will take at least four hours on high, or six to seven hours on low. A whole chicken, cut into pieces, will take about three hours on high and roughly five hours on low. Without the bones, chicken will take about an hour less.
- Dried pulses that have been previously boiled or soaked can be cooked for long periods; however, tinned vegetables should be added about an hour before you plan to serve.
- Check your food the first few times you experiment with your cooker. You may find it useful to have a thermometer to ensure that the food (and in particular meat) has reached the appropriate temperature. All slow cookers are different, and yours may be faster or slower than others.

The table below gives you an idea of how conventional and slow-cooking times differ, according to the heat setting.

Conventional oven (low)	Slow cooker (high)	Slow cooker (low)
15–30 minutes	1–2 hours	4–6 hours
35–40 minutes	3–4 hours	6–10 hours
50 minutes–3 hours	4–6 hours	8–18 hours

Slow cooking for health

One of the most positive benefits of slow cooking is the fact that the dishes you prepare tend to be much healthier than the traditionally cooked alternatives. First and foremost, everything you cook in the slow cooker is cooked in its own juices (or the liquid that you provide), which evaporates very little. This means that vitamins and minerals that are leached into the liquid while cooking are retained in the sauce or jus, rather than being discarded with the cooking water. Furthermore, food is usually cooked at a consistently low temperature, causing fewer nutrients to be destroyed in the process.

Many people find that they eat far more vegetables, and other healthy produce, such as pulses and wholegrains, because they are so easy to prepare in a slow cooker. Less meat is usually required for a satisfying meal because dishes can be easily bulked out with fresh vegetables and pulses such as lentils and beans.

In most cases, very little fat is used in a slow cooker, and by browning your meat in advance of cooking, you'll reduce the fat content further still. Simmering foods in light stocks, fruit juices and even alcohol with delicious herbs and spices gives them a wonderful flavour without the need for rich sauces or other fattening ingredients. Fresh vegetables and even fruit can be thrown in at the last minute, and literally steamed with the heat of the cooker's contents, to preserve nutrients and impart flavour without the use of fats.

Slow cookers also reduce the need to depend upon unhealthy prepackaged ready meals. Your home-cooked goodies will contain the amount of salt, sugar and fat that you decide to add. What's more, you can cook large quantities in a good-sized slow cooker and freeze the leftovers for another meal.

Another health-related advantage of slow cooking is that it is less likely to expose you to advanced glycation end products (AGEs) – toxins the body absorbs when we consume grilled, fried or broiled meats, cheeses and other foods of animal origin, and any foods cooked at high temperatures. AGEs may give food appetising tastes and smells, but in the body they have been linked to inflammation, insulin resistance, diabetes, vascular and kidney disease and Alzheimer's. The only way you can reduce your intake of AGEs is to cook at a low temperature and to maintain the water content of food.

Consider, too, the fact that many less expensive foods, such as tougher cuts of meat and meat on the bone, as well as pulses and grains, are actually the best for you. Their drawback is the cooking time they require, but with a slow cooker you can combine a variety of inexpensive, extremely healthy foods to create delicious, nutritious meals. Meat cooked on the bone, for example, releases calcium and other nutrients into the cooking juices, adding to your nutritional intake. Handfuls of lentils or soaked chickpeas can be thrown into the cooker for a Bvitamin burst; fibre-rich grains can be stirred into soups, casseroles and stews and left to absorb the fragrant flavours.

Slow-cooked meals can be much tastier than the conventional alternatives, so you may well be able to entice the faddier eaters in your family to try something new and healthy. Sprinkle finished dishes with chopped fresh herbs, lightly toasted seeds or nuts, a handful of goat's cheese or crumbled feta or some diced avocado or mango. The number of ways in which to include healthy foods is virtually limitless.

Cleaning your slow cooker

Keeping your slow cooker clean is important to ensure that you don't allow bacteria that can cause illness to breed (see opposite). Some models are easier to clean than others, so when you make your choice, go for one with a removable liner or 'pot' that can be immersed in hot, soapy water or even placed in the dishwasher. You can also purchase disposable liners which can be removed and discarded, so that you just need to wipe clean the interior of your cooker. Most are made of heat-resistant nylon and designed for easy clean-up. You may also wish to coat the inside of your pot with olive oil or a non-stick spray before use, to prevent food from sticking.

Use rubber or wooden utensils to avoid scratching the inside of the pot, which can then trap food debris and making cleaning more difficult. Use a soft cloth or brush when cleaning your pot; wire brushes or coarse sponges will scratch the inside.

When you've emptied the pot at serving time, fill it with hot, soapy water and soak for a while. The combination of soap and the residual heat from the cooker will make it easier to clean off any hardened or dried-on food. Let the slow cooker cool down a little before you wash it and don't add cold water to a hot slow cooker or put a hot slow cooker in cold water. The pot can crack or even break, rendering it useless.

The lid tends to require the most cleaning, as the cooking process forces the juices and other liquids up to the top of the pot. You may wish to soak this before using, or clean it on the top shelf of your dishwasher.

Wipe down the outside of the slow cooker with a damp cloth, and then dry completely. Make sure that it is never immersed in water. Take time to clean the cord too. Don't use abrasive cleaners, harsh chemicals or scouring pads on the outside of your cooker. Soaking the interior with a mild detergent, or a tablespoon of biological washing powder or liquid, will remove any difficult-to-shift stains or bits of food. Alternatively, try adding 250ml of white vinegar to your pot, and filling to about three-quarters with hot water. Cook with the cover on for about two hours, then decant the contents and rinse thoroughly.

Finally, dry completely before storing. This helps to stop a soap film from developing on the ceramic crock as well as preventing water stains from building up.

Slow cooking safety and hygiene

Well-maintained and carefully used slow cookers offer a safe and healthy alternative to conventional cooking. It is, however, important to be scrupulous about hygiene when cooking and preparing your dishes. Here's what you need to bear in mind:

- A slow cooker should cook slowly enough to allow the unit to be unattended (while you are at work, for example), but fast enough to ensure that food doesn't enter the 'bacteria' zone. In other words, food should remain above 60°C (140°F) to prevent bacteria from multiplying and potentially causing food-borne illness.
- If you have an old slow cooker, test to be sure that it reaches the temperature it needs to reach in order to kill bacteria. Fill it to about half full with tap water. Heat on the low setting for eight hours with the lid firmly on, then check the water temperature with an accurate food thermometer (quickly, as the temperature will drop rapidly when the lid is removed). The water should be at least 85°C (185°F). Temperatures below this would indicate your slow cooker neither heats food up hot enough nor fast enough to avoid potential food-safety problems.

- Make sure that you clean your work area and utensils before beginning food preparation. The slow cooker should also be scrupulously clean (see page 26).
- Make sure the slow cooker is sitting on a dry, stable surface. It must not lean on the wall or come into contact with other items on your kitchen bench.
- Before plugging in, have a good look at the plug and cord. Make sure there are no frays. Plug it firmly and directly into the outlet; avoid using extension cords.
- Before adding foods, check the inside of the cooker and don't use it if there are any chips, cracks or breaks.
- Ensure that all perishables (meat, vegetables, fish, etc.) are kept in the refrigerator until preparation times. Bacteria multiply at room temperature.
- Thoroughly defrost any frozen ingredients, but keep them in the refrigerator until you are ready to prepare them.
- Some experts recommend that you do not cook large joints or whole chickens in the slow cooker, because it will not reach a sufficiently high heat quickly enough to destroy bacteria; however, if you preheat the slow cooker and follow the instructions on pages 48 and 73, you can avoid potential problems. If you are worried, cut meat, poultry and vegetables into medium- to small-sized pieces to ensure that heat is rapidly transferred.
- Preheat the slow cooker before adding ingredients and cook on high for the first 60 minutes to ensure that the heat rises quickly enough to destroy bacteria.
- When cooking meat or poultry, the water or stock level should almost cover the ingredients to ensure effective heat transfer throughout the pot.
- Use an accurate food thermometer to test that your food is completely cooked. Poultry should be 82°C (180°F), pork 76°C (170°F) and beef 71°C (160°F).
- Do not leave cooked food to cool down in the slow cooker. Either consume it immediately, or place leftovers in shallow containers and refrigerate immediately. Avoid using your slow cooker to

reheat leftovers; you can, however, add them to the pot to form part of a meal that is (of course) slow cooked!

- Do not lift the lid or cover during the cooking cycle. Each time the lid is raised, the internal temperature drops.

2 Recipes

Once you've got the hang of slow cooking, you'll find it easy to adapt your favourite recipes. You'll be amazed by the number of different types of food that can be prepared this way. In this section you'll find a selection of tried-and-tested, delicious recipes designed to serve the whole family. If you wish to make a little less, simply reduce the quantities of each ingredient. But why not make a little extra and freeze what's left for another day?

Soups

Making soup in the slow cooker is simple. Whether you wish to throw in a few handfuls of leftovers to create a delicious concoction, use up vegetables that are approaching their use-by date, produce a hearty meal for your hungry family or create a sumptuous starter for an elegant dinner party, the slow cooker is at your service. What could be nicer than coming home to a big pot of hot soup, simmering away and ready to eat?

Using bones and carcasses from any meat and poultry, along with vegetable peelings and the stalks from herbs, you can make delicious stocks, too, which can be concentrated and frozen in ice-cube containers to use as required.

Top tips for successful soups

The flavours of the ingredients you include in the slow cooker will mingle and blend, then intensify as cooking continues. Therefore, you may not need as much seasoning or, indeed, stock, as you might think. Let your ingredients simmer away for a while, then taste for seasoning about an hour before you plan to eat. This still allows plenty of time to adjust your flavours and serve up the perfect soup. There are a few things to bear in mind when making soups:

- Always put root vegetables in the bottom of the pot, as they take the longest to cook. Cut them into small, uniformly sized pieces, so that they cook evenly.
- Softening vegetables before adding them to the pot helps to impart a rich flavour to the soup. Browning meat will do the same.
- If you are making soups without a recipe, you'll need about a litre (1¼ pints) of water for every four to six servings. If you are adding wine or any other liquid flavouring, add a little less stock or water.
- Soups can be thickened as they cook if meat is coated in seasoned flour before browning. Alternatively, blend together a few teaspoons of cornflour and a little water and stir until you have a milky, smooth paste, then stir in once your slow-cooking is bubbling.
- Most soups can be cooked on low for up to twelve hours without any ill-effects; however, six to eight hours is probably optimum time – or four to six hours on high.
- You can liquidise soups in the pot with a hand-held blender or, when they're ready, transfer to a liquidiser or food processor and blend until smooth. Return to the pot to keep warm until serving time.
- Remember that dairy produce such as cheese, sour cream, milk or yoghurt should not be added until the end of cooking time (see page 23). It's best to use cream, sour cream, crème fraîche or yoghurt as a garnish, and stir into the soup in a swirl just before serving.

Chunky Winter Vegetable Soup

This hearty soup is substantial enough to form the basis of a delicious winter meal, and you can add as many seasonal vegetables as you wish.

Serves 4–6
1 clove of garlic, whole
4 carrots, sliced
4 large white potatoes, peeled and sliced
1 parsnip, peeled and sliced
½ large squash, peeled and sliced
400g (14oz) tin chopped tomatoes
2 litres (3½ pints) hot vegetable stock
2 x 400g (14oz) tins mixed pulses, drained and rinsed
150g (6oz) spinach leaves
1 tbsp red pepper pesto
salt and pepper to taste

Lightly rub the inside of the slow cooker pot with olive oil, then rub with garlic clove. Crush the garlic clove and put to one side. Turn the slow cooker to high.

Layer the carrots, potatoes, parsnip and squash (and any other root vegetables you may wish to add) in the bottom of the pot. Cover with the chopped tomatoes, crushed garlic and hot stock and stir well. Bring the ingredients to a slow boil (about an hour), then turn down to low and cook for 6 to 8 hours. Tip in the pulses and the spinach and stir in the pesto. Cover and cook for another hour.

Just before serving, check seasoning and add salt and pepper as required.

Options
- Garnish with a swirl of crème fraîche and a handful of torn basil leaves.
- A grating of Parmesan cheese can be added at the last minute and stirred in to deepen the flavours.
- Top with toasted pine nuts before serving, for a little crunch.

Broccoli with Goat's Cheese Soup

This delicious soup makes an ideal lunch or starter. If you aren't keen on goat's cheese, substitute Brie or Camembert instead.

Serves 4–6
50g (1¾oz) butter
1 large onion, finely chopped
900g (2lb) broccoli, chopped into florets
generous grating of fresh nutmeg
1 litre (1¾ pints) hot chicken or vegetable stock
500ml (18fl oz) full-fat milk
salt and pepper to taste
100g (3½oz) soft goat's cheese, chopped

Preheat the slow cooker to high. In a large saucepan, melt the butter and gently soften the onions. Place in the bottom of your hot slow cooker, then tip in the broccoli. Add the grated nutmeg and cover with stock.

Cover and bring to a slow boil, then reduce the heat to low and cook for 6 to 8 hours. An hour before serving time, stir in the milk, then cover again.

Liquidise the soup just before serving. If desired, you can remove some of the broccoli with a slotted spoon, and stir into the soup once it has been puréed. Check seasoning and adjust as required. Scatter with the goat's cheese, and give it a gentle stir.

Options
• Serve with herby toasted croutons.
• Add a swirl of crème fraîche before serving, or some finely grated lemon zest.

Chorizo and Chickpea Soup

The robust flavours of the chorizo make this hearty soup a rich and warming treat all year round.

Serves 4–6
2 x 400g (14oz) tins chopped tomatoes
200g (7oz) chorizo sausage, cut into chunks
200g (7oz) Savoy cabbage, shredded
1 tsp dried chilli flakes
2 chicken or vegetable stock cubes
salt and pepper to taste
2 x 400g (14oz) tins chickpeas, drained and rinsed

Preheat the slow cooker to high, then tip in the tomatoes, sausage and cabbage. Stir in the dried chilli flakes and crumble the stock cubes over. Stir carefully and cover. Bring to a gentle boil, then reduce the heat to low. Cook for 6 to 8 hours. An hour before serving, check seasoning and adjust as necessary. Stir in the chickpeas and return to the heat.

Options
- Stir in a swirl of crème fraîche before serving and a handful of torn basil leaves.
- Chicken makes a good addition to this soup. Simply stir in a couple of handfuls of pre-cooked chicken, cut into chunks, when you add the chickpeas.

Thai Chicken and Coconut Soup

This creamy soup is bursting with Eastern flavours and can be served with rice for a delicious Thai meal.

Serves 4–6
2 x 400g (14oz) tins coconut milk
3 tbsp fish sauce
4cm (1½in) piece fresh ginger, peeled and finely chopped
6 kaffir lime leaves
1 fresh red chilli, chopped
2 tsp light brown sugar
1 lemongrass stalk, bashed
500g (1lb 2oz) boneless, skinless chicken breasts, cut into small pieces
2 tbsp lime juice
salt and pepper to taste
handful of fresh basil leaves, torn
handful of fresh coriander, roughly chopped

Preheat the slow cooker to high. When hot, add the coconut milk, fish sauce, ginger, lime leaves, chilli, sugar and lemongrass. Cover and simmer for about an hour on high, then add the chicken. Reduce the heat to low, cover and cook for 6 to 8 hours.

About 30 minutes before serving, stir in the lime juice, check seasoning and adjust as necessary. Replace the lid and continue cooking.

Remove the lid, stir in the herbs and ladle into bowls.

Options
- Prawns can be used instead of chicken, but should be added 30 minutes before serving. If using frozen prawns, make sure they are defrosted thoroughly before adding.

Tomato and Basil Soup

This soup is really easy to make and is delicious served warm or cold. Use it as a base for vegetable soups, stirring in leftover vegetables for the last hour or so of cooking time.

Serves 4–6
2 tbsp olive oil
1 onion, finely chopped
1 carrot, finely chopped
1 celery stick, finely chopped
2 tsp tomato purée
1kg (2lb 4oz) ripe tomatoes, quartered
1 bay leaf
1 tsp dried basil
pinch of sugar
1.2 litres (2 pints) vegetable stock
salt and pepper to taste
2 handfuls of fresh basil leaves, torn

Preheat the slow cooker to high. In a large saucepan, heat the oil and gently soften the onion, carrot and celery. This should take about 10 minutes.

When the slow cooker is hot, tip the softened vegetables into the bottom, stir in the tomato purée and tip in the tomatoes. Add the bay leaf, dried basil and sugar and cover with the vegetable stock. Cover and heat on high for about 30 minutes. Turn down the heat and cook for 5 to 7 hours on low.

About 30 minutes before serving, check seasoning and adjust as necessary. At the end of cooking time, purée the soup with a hand-held blender in the slow cooker. You may then wish to pour it through a sieve to remove any tomato skins. Serve immediately, garnished with torn basil leaves.

Options

- If serving cold, leave the soup to cool and then refrigerate for a couple of hours.
- Dice fresh mozzarella and avocado, and use along with the basil for a garnish.
- A swirl of fresh yoghurt or crème fraîche adds a pretty and delicious finishing touch.
- Transform your soup into a Tuscan Bean Soup. Lightly fry 1 small red onion (finely chopped), 1 clove of garlic (crushed), 1 carrot (peeled and diced), and 5 sundried tomatoes (finely chopped) in a little olive oil until the onion is soft. Add to your Tomato and Basil Soup in the slow cooker, along with a 400g can mixed beans (drained and rinsed), 2 tsp thyme and 1 tsp sundried tomato paste. Continue cooking on high for a further 2 hours, until the carrots are tender to the touch. Serve with a dollop of green pesto.

Hearty Minestrone

You can use any combination of vegetables in this soup, but be sure to add anything that was previously frozen in the last hour or so of cooking. This hearty soup makes a substantial meal, served with a fresh green salad and some crusty bread.

Serves 4–6
1 tbsp olive oil
3 streaky bacon rashers, finely chopped (alternatively, use 6 tbsp bacon lardons)
1 medium onion, finely chopped
2 medium carrots, finely chopped
1 leek, washed, trimmed and thinly sliced
2 celery sticks, thinly sliced
100g (3½oz) white cabbage, shredded
1 clove of garlic, crushed
1 litre (1¾ pints) chicken stock
4 tbsp tomato purée
400g (14oz) tin chopped tomatoes
1 bay leaf
1 tsp dried thyme
1 tsp dried basil
1 tsp dried oregano
50g (1¾oz) dried macaroni or other small pasta shapes
salt and pepper to taste
freshly grated Parmesan cheese

Preheat the slow cooker to high. Heat the oil in a large saucepan and add the bacon. Cook until just brown, then add the onion, carrots, leek, celery, cabbage and garlic. Cook for 3 to 4 minutes.

Tip into the pot of the slow cooker, then stir in the stock, tomato purée, tomatoes, bay leaf, thyme, basil and oregano. Reduce the heat and cook for 6 to 8 hours on low. About 60 minutes before serving, add the dried macaroni or other pasta.

Check seasoning and adjust as necessary. Serve with grated Parmesan cheese on top.

Options

- Brown bite-sized chunks of casserole beef along with the bacon and cook as usual, for a delicious stew.
- If you are pushed for time, add pre-cooked macaroni or another pasta shape about 30 minutes before serving.
- A handful of mature Cheddar cheese, grated, can be used in place of the Parmesan for a rich, melty topping.
- About 60 minutes before serving, throw in a handful of green beans, peas, or any leftover green vegetables.

Summer Soup with Pesto

This light soup is surprisingly filling, and perfect for those balmy summer evenings. You can use any summery green vegetables.

Serves 4–6
2 courgettes, halved and very thinly sliced
200g (7oz) frozen peas, defrosted
600ml (1 pint) chicken or vegetable stock
1 bay leaf
100g (3½oz) baby spinach
4 tbsp pesto
250g (9oz) basmati rice that has been pre-cooked
grated Parmesan cheese, to sprinkle
olive oil, to drizzle

Preheat the slow cooker to high, then layer the courgette slices in the bottom. Top with peas and vegetable stock, then add the bay leaf. Cook on high for 30 minutes, then reduce the heat to low and cook for 5 to 6 hours. An hour before serving time, stir in the spinach, pesto and rice.

To serve, decant into bowls and sprinkle with Parmesan and a drizzle of olive oil.

Options
• Add the grated zest of one lime when you add the spinach, pesto and rice, for a fresh, summery flavour.

Smoked Haddock Chowder

This nourishing soup is rich and satisfying, and best served piping hot from the slow cooker.

Serves 4–6
1 large onion, chopped
3 medium white potatoes, scrubbed and cubed
good grating of fresh nutmeg
pinch of chilli powder
1 litre (1¾ pints) hot vegetable stock
400g (14oz) tin sweetcorn, drained
400g (14oz) tin evaporated milk
4 smoked haddock fillets (about 100g/3½oz each), cut into chunks
salt and pepper to taste
2 handfuls of parsley, chopped

Preheat the slow cooker until hot. Layer the onion and potatoes in the bottom of the pot and sprinkle over the grated nutmeg. Sprinkle with chilli powder and cover with the stock. Cover and bring to the boil. Reduce the heat to low, then tip in the sweetcorn and the evaporated milk. Cook for 5 to 6 hours.

About 30 to 45 minutes before serving, stir in the haddock and add salt and pepper to taste. Continue cooking. To serve, stir in the parsley and ladle into bowls.

Options
- Stir in a teaspoon of fresh lemon zest with the haddock, to give a delicious lemony scent to your soup.

Chicken and Chestnut Soup

The chestnuts give a nutty sweetness to this soup, but if you find them difficult to get hold of, it works perfectly well without them. This is a rich and filling soup – perfect for a special occasion.

Serves 6
30g (1oz) butter
1 medium onion, chopped
4 celery sticks, chopped
2 carrots, chopped
2 cloves of garlic, crushed
juice and zest of 1 lemon
1 tsp ground allspice
1 bay leaf
1 litre (1¾ pints) hot chicken stock
50g (1¾oz) pearl barley
250g (9oz) cooked chicken
80ml (3fl oz) white wine or sherry
80ml (3fl oz) double cream
100g (3½oz) whole chestnuts, peeled, cooked and chopped
2 handfuls of frozen green beans, defrosted
small handful of parsley, chopped
salt and pepper to taste

Preheat the slow cooker to high. In a large saucepan, melt the butter and gently soften the onion, celery, carrots and garlic. Place in the bottom of the slow cooker and add the lemon juice and zest, allspice and bay leaf. Top with hot chicken stock and stir in the pearl barley. Cover, bring to the boil, then reduce the heat to low. Cook for 6 to 8 hours.

An hour before serving time, stir in the chicken, wine, cream, chestnuts and green beans. Replace the lid and resume cooking.

Before serving, stir in the parsley and add salt and pepper to taste.

Options

- Pheasant or any other rich poultry can be used in place of chicken.
- For a smooth, creamy soup, leave out the barley and purée before serving.
- A fresh garnish of watercress works well with this soup.
- To add extra crunch and bring out the flavours of this rich soup, gently fry thinly sliced peel from half a lemon, along with 1 tsp sherry, a handful of finely chopped chestnuts, one thinly sliced garlic clove, 2 tbsp chopped onion in about 1 tbsp butter. Cook over medium heat, stirring frequently, until the onions are soft and slightly browned. Place a little at the bottom of each soup bowl before ladling in the warm soup. Alternatively, you can sprinkle a little over the top of each bowl before serving.

Creamy Carrot and Lemon Soup

This soup is so easy to make, it will become a household staple. Serve it warm or cold.

Serves 4–6
1 tbsp sunflower oil
1 onion, peeled and sliced
1 clove of garlic, peeled and crushed
600g (1lb 5oz) carrots, peeled and chopped
1 litre (1¾ pints) vegetable stock
zest and juice of 1 lemon
salt and pepper to taste
handful of fresh parsley, chopped
extra strips of lemon zest, to garnish

Preheat the slow cooker to high. In a large saucepan, heat the sunflower oil and soften the onion and garlic. Place in the bottom of the hot slow cooker and cover with the carrots. Pour over the stock and add the lemon zest. Bring to the boil, then reduce the heat to low. Cook for 5 to 6 hours.

Half an hour before serving, stir in the lemon juice and season to taste. When you are ready to serve, use a hand-held blender to liquidise the soup. Serve with a strip of lemon zest and a handful of parsley.

Options
- Stir in 2 tsp dried coriander when you add the lemon juice, and garnish with fresh coriander.
- Use orange zest and juice in place of lemon, if you wish.

Polish Sausage and Cabbage Soup

A simple, but satisfying soup that is unbelievably easy to make, using a type of Polish sausage known as kielbasa.

Serves 4–6
30g (1oz) butter
2 medium onions, diced
4 celery sticks, chopped
12 small new potatoes (red, if you can get them)
½ medium white cabbage, shredded
500g (1lb 2oz) baby carrots
1kg (2¼lb) kielbasa, diced
2 tsp caraway seeds
1 litre (1¾ pints) hot chicken or vegetable stock
salt and pepper to taste

Preheat the slow cooker to high. In a saucepan, melt the butter and soften the onions and celery for about 5 minutes. Tip into the hot slow cooker, along with the potatoes, cabbage, carrots, sausage and caraway seeds. Cover with the stock. Bring to the boil, then reduce the heat to low. Cook for 6 to 8 hours. Just before serving, check seasoning and adjust as necessary.

Options
- Serve with warm crusty bread.
- Kielbasa is available in most supermarkets and delicatessens but if you can't find it, any pre-cooked pork or beef sausage will do.

Lemon, Spinach and Lentil Soup

This dish has Moroccan overtones and is delightfully fresh and fragrant.

Serves 6
3 tbsp olive oil
2 medium onions, finely chopped
4 cloves of garlic, minced
2 tsp ground cumin
½ tsp cayenne pepper
300g (10½oz) green or brown lentils, rinsed
1 litre (1¾ pints) vegetable or chicken stock
450ml (15fl oz) water
2 tsp dried mint
zest and juice of 2 lemons
200g (7oz) spinach, washed and stems removed
salt and pepper to taste
plain yoghurt, to garnish
mint leaves, optional

Preheat the slow cooker to high. In a large saucepan, heat the olive oil and add the onions. Cook until softened. Stir in the garlic and cook for another minute or so. Add to the slow cooker, along with the cumin, cayenne pepper, lentils, stock, water and mint. Bring to the boil, then reduce the heat and simmer on low for 5 to 7 hours.

Stir in the lemon zest and juice and spinach. Cover and cook for another 30 to 60 minutes, then season to taste. Ladle into warm bowls and garnish with a dollop of yoghurt and, if desired, some fresh mint leaves.

Options
- This soup can be puréed before serving, for a creamier texture.
- Replace the cumin with dried coriander leaves and omit the mint, for a more Eastern flavour.

Super Stock

You can create a delicious stock from leftover bones (chicken, fish, lamb and beef) and any combination of seasoning can be added. Simply place everything in the slow cooker, cover, cook, strain and you are ready to go! Don't hesitate to throw in leftover vegetables, or even peelings, to make your stock even more flavourful.

For chicken stock, use the bones or carcass of 1 chicken and add:
2 tsp dried tarragon
1 tsp dried basil
1 tsp dried chervil
1 tbsp dried parsley
5 black peppercorns
1 tsp white wine vinegar
1 bay leaf
1 carrot, chopped
1 celery stick, chopped
1 onion or leek, chopped
1.5 litres (2½ pints) boiling water

Place all the ingredients in the slow cooker, cook on high for 8 to 10 hours, then strain. If you wish, you can then return the stock to the pot and continue to cook with the lid off for several hours to make the stock more concentrated. Store in the fridge for up to two weeks, or freeze in ice-cube trays to use as required.

Options
- Use the above as a base for all stocks, substituting herbs and spices as desired. You can create 'Thai' or 'Indian' stocks or add Mediterranean herbs and spices along with tomatoes for a richer stock. For fish stock, try dill, parsley, white wine and a fresh fennel bulb. For lamb stock, use dried mint, rosemary, garlic and thyme. For beef stock, try oregano, mustard powder, garlic, red wine and tomatoes.

Meat

Preparing meat in the slow cooker couldn't be easier and, as long as you choose cuts with a good marbling or cover of fat, you are guaranteed a tasty, melt-in-the-mouth meal. The longer you cook your meat, the more tender it will be. You can enhance the flavour by marinating overnight.

Slow-cooked roasts

Roasting meat in a slow cooker is surprisingly easy, as long as you have plenty of time to let it cook in its own juices. If you wish, you can add vegetables too, to ensure that everything all elements of the meal are ready at the same time.

There are a few things to bear in mind when using the slow cooker to roast meat:

- Choose a joint that fits easily inside the slow cooker. The lid will need to fit firmly on top, and there should be at least a centimetre between the top of the roast and the lid.
- Trim off excess fat and brown meat. This is not essential, but browning ensures that your roast has a healthy colour when finished, rather than looking slightly wan or grey.
- No liquid is required when roasting in the slow cooker; however, you can choose to add a little lemon juice or wine, for example, to impart some flavour.
- Onions, herbs, spices and even a lemon can be placed on or around the joint to give added flavour.
- Whole joints of pork should always be cooked on high, and will take between three and five hours, depending on size.
- Beef and other meats can be cooked on high or low. They will require four to ten hours of cooking on lower settings, depending on the size of the joint, and about three to six hours on high.

Generally speaking, a 1.6kg (3½lb) roast will need three to six hours, while a 2.25kg (5lb) roast will need between five and eight. The variations in time reflect the difference in slow cookers, all of which cook things at their own pace, as well as the cut of meat you are using.

- You may wish to check your joint about four hours into cooking to ensure that it is cooking evenly.
- The roast is done when meat falls from the bone, or can be cut easily with a butter knife.
- Don't expect your roast to be the same as it would be if you'd cooked it in the oven. The meat will be tender and moist – and much softer.

Best cuts of meat for slow cooking

Even cooking at the slow cooker's highest heat can produce extremely tender meat because the temperature will still be cool enough to convert the connective tissue in the meat slowly from collagen to gelatine, making it mouth-wateringly moist. What's more, the cheaper cuts of meat tend to contain the most collagen, which is a bonus if you are on a tight budget.

Some of the best cuts to look out for will be labelled 'braising', 'stewing' or 'casserole', and, in particular, you can look out for shanks, knuckles, brisket, shoulder, rump, round and skirt. Ironically, the more expensive cuts, such as sirloin, do not work as well in a slow cooker as they can end up losing their texture.

If you are choosing beef, look for cuts from the shoulder or 'chuck', such as rib roasts, blade roasts, brisket, short ribs, oxtail and stewing or casserole beef. Pork shoulder cuts are best, such as blade roasts or steaks; rib roasts and rib chops also work well. Lamb shoulder and shanks are the best, and if you are cooking poultry, go for the legs and thighs, which remain the moistest and the most appetising in your slowcooker. See the chart on pages 151–54 for further advice on the best cuts of meat to use for particular dishes.

Preparing meat for slow cooking

One of the best things about slow cooking is the minimal preparation required. Apart from some cutting and seasoning, you'll need to do very little to the meat you use. Even marinating isn't strictly necessary as the meat will effectively be marinating as it slow cooks in its own juices. There are, however, a few things to bear in mind when preparing meat for the slow cooker:

- There are many advantages to cutting the meat yourself. Not only will you pay a premium for having it diced or cut in the supermarket or at the butcher, but you may end up paying for a lot of fat and gristle that you don't want. Cutting meat at home will allow you to make all the pieces a uniform size (to ensure even cooking) and also to trim off unwanted bits.
- Roughly speaking, 2½cm (1in) cubes of meat are ideal for slow cooking, mainly because the meat will finish cooking at the same as the vegetables you use.
- Browning adds a rich colour to the meat and the finished sauces or gravy. It's less important for lighter-coloured meats such as pork, veal and chicken, because they absorb colour from the sauce to some extent, but is recommended for ground or minced meat to prevent it from clumping and to get rid of excess fat. Browning can be undertaken in a pan or under the grill, and it does help to bring out the flavour. Before browning, coat meat in seasoned flour, which also helps to thicken sauces and gravies.
- Always use the juices created when you brown your meat, by adding them to the slow cooker along with the meat. Many flavours are concentrated there.
- Rub meat with dried herbs and spices to create more powerful flavours, or poke garlic, spices and herbs into slits cut into the surface of the meat itself.

Thai Beef Curry

This flavoursome dish is about as simple as it gets! Serve with sticky, fragrant jasmine rice.

Serves 4–6
1kg (2¼lb) casserole beef, diced
500ml (18fl oz) coconut milk
2 tbsp Thai red curry paste
4 tbsp fish sauce
3 tbsp brown sugar
2 handfuls of fresh coriander
200g (7oz) tin water chestnuts, drained

Preheat the slow cooker. When hot, place the beef in the bottom. Whisk together the coconut milk, curry paste, fish sauce and brown sugar and pour over the meat. Cook on high for about 30 minutes, then reduce the heat to low. Cook for 6 to 8 hours, stirring in half of the coriander and the drained water chestnuts about 30 minutes before serving time.

Serve, garnished with the remaining coriander.

Options
- Add some cubed, cooked potatoes or stir in some green beans, about 30 minutes before the end of cooking time.
- Butternut squash makes a nice addition – cut into 2½cm (1in) cubes and add once the slow cooker is hot.

Italian Meatball Casserole

I love this hearty rustic dish. Serve it in big bowls with rice or pasta – or even just a chunk of granary bread.

Serves 4–6
For the meatballs
3 tbsp chopped onion
6 tbsp dried breadcrumbs
3 tbsp milk
500g (1lb 2oz) beef or pork mince
small bunch of parsley, chopped
1 tsp dried oregano
1 tsp dried basil
salt and pepper
1 tbsp olive oil

For the sauce
2 large onions, chopped
2 cloves of garlic, crushed
450g (1lb) carrots, cut into chunks
450g (1lb) white potatoes, peeled and cut into chunks
1 tbsp paprika
1 tbsp dried thyme
500g (1lb 2oz) jar of passata (creamed tomatoes)

Preheat the slow cooker to high. Soak the chopped onion and bread-crumbs in the milk, and mix with the beef or pork, parsley, oregano and basil, as well as salt and pepper to taste. Shape into small balls.

Heat the olive oil in a large frying pan, and fry the meatballs for 4 to 5 minutes, turning frequently to ensure that they are brown all over.

Next, place the onions, garlic, carrots and potatoes in the bottom of the slow cooker and cover with the meatballs. Pour over about 300ml (10fl oz) water and stir in the paprika, thyme and passata. Cover and bring to the boil on high, then turn down the heat to low and cook for 5 to 6 hours.

Serve in big bowls with pasta or rice, or on their own.

Options

- Sprinkle with Parmesan cheese and fresh oregano for an authentic Italian flavour.
- Beef works equally well in meatballs, but can be a little tougher when cooked. A blend of beef and pork is perfect.
- If desired, use minced turkey or chicken in place of beef or pork, and substitute 1 tsp tarragon for the oregano for a lighter, fresher taste. Sprinkle with fresh parsley and freshly grated Parmesan cheese, and a leaf or two of fresh, chopped tarragon, before serving.
- For a richer, heartier sauce, stir in 1 tbsp sundried tomato paste with the paprika, thyme and passata and about 60 minutes before serving, add 3 tbsp chopped sundried tomatoes and a small bottle of artichoke hearts in oil, drained and chopped into chunks.

Zesty Ham and Beans

This one-pot meal is perfect for cold winter evenings or served cool in the garden for summer.

Serves 4–6
2 tbsp olive oil
1 large onion, chopped
2 celery sticks, chopped
450g (1lb) gammon, cut into large chunks
250g (9oz) dried haricot beans, soaked overnight
zest and juice of 2 oranges
zest and juice of 1 lemon
1 tbsp paprika
3 tbsp dark brown sugar
1 tbsp black treacle or molasses
500ml (18fl oz) vegetable or chicken stock
2 tbsp white wine vinegar
3 tbsp tomato purée
pinch of cinnamon
4 whole cloves
200g (7oz) tin mandarin oranges
salt and pepper to taste

Preheat the slow cooker to high. In a large saucepan, heat the oil and soften the onion and celery. Place in the bottom of the slow cooker, then top with the gammon. Drain the beans and pour over the gammon. Next, mix together the orange and lemon zests and juices with the paprika, sugar, treacle, stock, vinegar, tomato purée, cinnamon and cloves, and pour over the ham and beans. Cover and bring to the boil, then reduce the heat to low and cook for 6 to 8 hours.

Remove the lid, stir in the mandarin oranges and continue cooking for another hour. Season to taste, and serve.

Traditional Beef Pot Roast

There can be nothing more delicious and satisfying than a slow-cooked pot roast, nestling in a rich gravy, surrounded by tender vegetables.

Serves 4–6
beef joint, about 1kg (2¼lb)
salt and pepper
12 new potatoes, halved
2 large carrots, peeled and cut into chunks
2 celery sticks, sliced
1 medium onion, sliced
1 large parsnip, peeled and sliced
2 bay leaves
1 tsp dried rosemary
1 tsp dried thyme
240ml (8fl oz) beef stock
150ml (5fl oz) red wine

Preheat the slow cooker to high. Trim excess fat from the beef and discard. Rub salt and pepper into the beef and set aside. Combine potatoes, carrots, celery, onion, parsnip and all of the seasoning in the slow cooker, then place the meat on top. Pour the stock over the top, then pour over the red wine. Cover and cook on high for 60 minutes, then turn down the heat and cook on low for about 9 hours, or until beef pulls apart easily when pressed with a fork.

Options
- If you want to make a gravy, remove the beef and vegetables with a slotted spoon and keep warm in the oven. Then mix 2 tbsp cornflour with a little water to make a milky liquid and pour into a saucepan with the juices from the slow cooker. Bring to the boil and stir constantly until it reaches the desired consistency.

Lamb Tagine with Dried Fruit

This traditional North African dish has lots of ingredients, but little preparation is required. Simply assemble everything in the slow cooker, and serve with cous-cous or rice.

Serves 4–6
4 tsp ground cumin
2 tsp ground turmeric
2 tsp salt
½ tsp pepper
½ tsp smoked paprika
½ tsp chilli powder
1½kg (3lb 5oz) boneless, trimmed lamb shoulder, cut into 5cm (2in) cubes
50g (1¾oz) plain flour
2 tbsp oil
2 large onions, sliced
4 tsp chopped garlic
1 tbsp ginger, finely chopped
100g (3½oz) dried apricots
100g (3½oz) raisins
1 tbsp honey
2–3 cinnamon sticks
850ml (30fl oz) vegetable stock
100g (3½oz) pitted dates

Preheat the slow cooker to high. Stir together the cumin, turmeric, salt, pepper, paprika and chilli, then add the cubed lamb. Sprinkle with 45g of the flour, and toss.

In a large saucepan, heat the oil and add the lamb, browning on all sides. Remove with a slotted spoon, then add the onions, frying until just soft.

Place the onions in the bottom of the slow cooker. Stir together the garlic, ginger, apricots, raisins, honey, cinnamon sticks and stock, and pour over the onions. Next, place the lamb pieces on top, sprinkling over the remaining flour.

Cover and cook on high for 2 hours. Then, quickly stir in the dates and reduce the heat to low. Cook for 5 hours or until the lamb is tender when pressed with a fork. Serve immediately.

Options
- Substitute green or brown olives for the dried fruit in this recipe, but add them in the last hour of cooking.
- This works nicely with the addition of 2 or 3 preserved, thinly sliced lemons.
- Top with toasted almonds.

Braised Pork with Apples

This unbelievably tender pork dish is perfectly accompanied by the apples, which are cooked and sieved to create a light and slightly tart sauce. Ideally, the meat should be marinated overnight, but if you are too busy, it will still taste delicious cooked straight away.

Serves 4–6
3kg (6½lb) boneless pork shoulder
1 tbsp fennel seeds, toasted and finely ground
2 tsp black peppercorns, cracked
2 tbsp dried thyme
2 tbsp fresh rosemary leaves, roughly chopped
4 medium cloves of garlic, crushed
2 tbsp salt
4 tbsp olive oil
4–5 large cooking apples, washed, peeled, cored and cut into eighths
1 large onion, chopped
salt and pepper

Trim the pork and pat it dry.

Mix together the toasted fennel seeds, cracked peppercorns, thyme, rosemary leaves, garlic, salt and half the olive oil. Rub the mixture evenly over the pork shoulder, inside and out. Wrap the pork shoulder tightly in plastic wrap to hold the marinade against the skin and marinate overnight. (If you are too busy to do this in advance, just go ahead and cook it.)

Preheat the slow cooker to high. Place the apple and onion chunks in a bowl with the remaining olive oil and season with salt and pepper. Place in the bottom of the slow cooker and put the marinated pork shoulder on top. Cover and cook on high for about 6 to 7 hours. When the pork is very tender and pulls apart easily when probed with a fork, remove it from the cooker.

Next, place the pan juices together with the cooked apples and onions in a liquidiser (or use a hand-held blender) to create a purée. Strain to remove any hard bits and serve alongside the pork.

Options

- Cut up a bulb of fennel and omit the onions, mixing together the apples and fennel instead, to create a fresh, aniseed flavour.
- For a festive roast, substitute the 4–5 cooking apples with 2 slightly under-ripe pears (peeled, cored and roughly chopped), 2 cooking apples (peeled, cored and roughly chopped), a handful each of dried cranberries and dried sour cherries, along with 1 tsp mixed spice. Follow the recipe instructions, mashing rather than puréeing the sauce to serve alongside the roast. Sprinkle with toasted pecan nuts for flavour and crunch.

Lucky Irish Stew with Dumplings

What better way to celebrate St Patrick's Day than with this easy, delicious stew. Add a few more potatoes and carrots if you are feeding a crowd!

Serves 4–6
For the stew
1kg (2¼lb) stewing or casserole beef, cut into cubes
150g (5½oz) flour
1 tsp salt
2 tbsp olive oil
4 carrots, peeled and chopped
2 small swedes, peeled and chopped
1 large onion, chopped
500g (1lb 2oz) white potatoes, cut into chunks
700ml (25fl oz) boiling vegetable or beef stock
salt and pepper to taste

For the dumplings
60g (2oz) plain flour
¼ tsp salt
¾ tsp baking powder
¾ tbsp shortening, lard or baking margarine
70ml (2½fl oz) milk

Preheat the slow cooker to high. Toss beef cubes in a mixture of the flour and salt and brown in the olive oil.

Place the vegetables in the bottom of the slow cooker. Cover with the beef, pour over the stock and cook on high for 30 minutes. Reduce the heat and cook on low for another 7 to 8 hours. The beef should fall apart at the touch of a fork.

To make the dumplings, sift together the flour, salt and baking powder. Using a knife or the back of a fork, cut in your shortening (see page 156 for instructions) and stir in the milk until smooth. Drop by the tablespoonful on to the hot stew, then cover and cook for another 60 minutes.

Options

- Stir some chopped chives into your dumpling batter to give them more flavour.
- If you like a little more bite to your stews, mix in a teaspoon each of paprika and mild chilli powder with the vegetables.
- A good grating of Parmesan cheese or a handful of grated mature Cheddar cheese will add flavour and substance to your dumplings. Simply stir into the batter and cook as usual. Alternatively, you can sprinkle the cheese over the dumplings about 30 minutes before serving, for a melt-in-your-mouth treat.

Sausage and Cannellini Bean Stew

This Italian-inspired dish is bursting with flavour. Serve it with a fresh green salad and polenta for an authentic Italian experience.

Serves 4–6
1 tbsp olive oil
500g (1lb 2oz) lean beef chipolata sausages
200g (7oz) streaky bacon or pancetta, diced
1 large red onion, chopped
2 cloves of garlic, crushed
1 small red chilli, deseeded and finely chopped
2 tsp sweet paprika
400g (14oz) tin chopped tomatoes
300ml (10fl oz) beef stock
1 tbsp tomato paste
400g (14oz) tin cannellini beans, rinsed and drained
handful of flat-leaf parsley leaves, chopped, to serve

Preheat the slow cooker to high. Heat the oil in a heavy-based saucepan and add the sausages, cooking for about 4 minutes until browned. Remove from the pan and set aside. Add the bacon, onion, garlic and chilli to the pan and cook for about 2 minutes.

Place the onion and bacon mixture in the bottom of the slow cooker, then top with the sausages. Mix together the paprika and the chopped tomatoes and pour over the sausages. Mix together the beef stock and the tomato paste, and add that too. Cook on high for 30 minutes, then reduce the heat to low. Cook for about 6 hours.

An hour before serving, tip in the cannellini beans, then replace the lid.

Serve stew in big bowls on top of polenta (if using) and garnished with flat-leaf parsley.

Options
- Butter or pinto beans can be substituted, if desired. And pork sausages work just as well as beef.

Bolognese Sauce

This is a tasty sauce that is excellent served on spaghetti or other types of pasta, or in jacket potatoes.

Serves 4–6
1 tbsp olive oil
100g (3½oz) streaky bacon, cut into small pieces
685g (1½lb) lean minced beef
1 large onion, finely chopped
2 celery sticks, finely chopped
1 carrot, finely chopped
2 cloves of garlic, crushed
400g (14oz) tin chopped tomatoes
2 tbsp tomato purée
150ml (5fl oz) beef stock
1 tbsp thyme
80ml (2¾fl oz) red wine
salt and pepper to taste

Preheat the slow cooker to high. In a large saucepan, heat the oil and add the bacon and beef, cooking until brown. Remove with a slotted spoon and place in the bottom of the slow cooker. Next, add the onion, celery, carrot and garlic to the pan and cook on low heat for about 6 minutes, or until the onion is slightly softened. Stir into the beef and bacon in the slow cooker.

Add the tomatoes, tomato purée, beef stock, thyme and wine and stir into the slow cooker. Cover and cook on low for 5 to 8 hours. Stir well and season to taste before serving.

Options
- Add some red kidney beans and a few teaspoons of chilli powder for an almost instant chilli con carne.

Moussaka

This traditional Greek dish can be made using lamb or beef. Balance the richness by serving with a lemon-dressed, fresh green salad and/or a dollop of tsatziki.

Serves 4–6
olive oil for greasing
2 medium aubergines, thinly sliced
salt and pepper
2 tsp olive oil
450g (1lb) lean minced lamb or beef
1 medium onion, finely chopped
2 cloves of garlic, crushed
½ tsp ground nutmeg
1 tsp ground cinnamon
1 tsp dried oregano
150ml (5fl oz) lamb or beef stock
2 tbsp tomato purée
30g (1oz) butter
30g (1oz) corn flour
600ml (1 pint) milk
Parmesan or mature Cheddar cheese, grated

Grease the inside of the slow cooker, then place the aubergines over the base. Season each layer with some salt and pepper.

Heat the oil in a frying pan, and brown the mince. Add the onion and garlic and cook for a further minute or two. Season lightly and add the nutmeg, cinnamon, oregano, stock and tomato purée. Bring to the boil, then spoon over the aubergines.

In a small saucepan, melt the butter and stir in the cornflour to make a roux. Cook gently until thick, then slowly add the milk, stirring constantly. When you have a nice, thick white sauce, remove from the heat and pour over the top of the lamb base. Cover and cook on low for 6 to 9 hours.

If you have a removable pot, sprinkle with grated cheese and place under the grill until brown.

Options

- Crumble some feta cheese into the white sauce for an authentic flavour, or use instead of Parmesan on top.
- Very thinly sliced potatoes can be alternated with the aubergines to form the bottom layers of the dish.
- To make your own tsatziki, simply add a handful each of finely chopped fresh mint, finely chopped fresh coriander, finely chopped fresh dill, half of one cucumber, chopped, 1 finely chopped garlic clove and salt and pepper to taste, to 200ml (7fl oz) Greek yoghurt. Stir together and cool for at least an hour to allow the flavours to merge.

Meaty Hungarian Goulash

This dish is simple, with no browning required. Serve with rice or a chunk of fresh crusty bread.

Serves 4–6
1 large onion, cut into chunks
1 large green pepper, cut into chunks
3 cloves of garlic, crushed
800g (1¾lb) diced braising steak
1 tbsp plain flour
2 tbsp sweet paprika
570g (1¼lb) jar passata
150ml (5fl oz) red wine
salt and pepper to taste
crème fraîche or sour cream to serve

Preheat the slow cooker to high. Place the onion, green pepper, garlic, steak, flour and paprika in a large bowl and mix it all together with your hands. Place in the slow cooker, then stir in the wine and passata. Cover and cook for 8 hours on low, or until the beef is tender.

Season to taste and serve in tureens with a swirl of crème fraîche on each and a sprinkling of paprika.

Options
- Although it isn't traditional, you can substitute chicken thighs for the beef.
- Why not use your goulash as a tasty topping for baked potatoes?

Chinese Braised Lamb

This is essentially a lamb stew with Chinese seasoning and flavours. It takes a little while to prepare, but once in the pot it's just a case of leaving it to its own devices.

Serves 4–6
1 tbsp olive oil
1.4 kg (3lb) lamb shoulder, boned and cubed
2 medium onions, chopped
4 cloves of garlic, crushed
2 green peppers, finely sliced
5cm (2in) piece of fresh ginger, peeled and thinly sliced
450ml (15fl oz) lamb or chicken stock
50g (1¾oz) light brown soft sugar
3 tbsp light soy sauce
½ cinnamon stick
2 star anise
2 tbsp smooth peanut butter
1 tbsp either hoisin or plum sauce
4 spring onions, finely sliced

Preheat the slow cooker. In a large saucepan, heat the oil and brown the lamb. Remove with a slotted spoon and set aside. Add the onions, garlic, peppers and ginger to the pan and fry for about 5 minutes. Place the onion and pepper mixture in the bottom of the slow cooker, and place the lamb on top. Mix together the stock, sugar, soy sauce, cinnamon, star anise, peanut butter and hoisin sauce, and pour over the lamb. Cover and bring to the boil, then reduce the heat to low and cook for 8 to 10 hours.

Serve with egg noodles (or rice), garnished with lots of finely sliced spring onions and perhaps a side dish of pak choi.

Options
- Drain a small (200g/7oz) tin of water chestnuts or bamboo shoots and stir in for added crunch.

Steak and Kidney Pudding

Steamed puddings work beautifully in a slow cooker, and this is no exception. You'll need a large pudding basin (about 1 litre/1¾ pints) for this dish, but check that it will fit into your slow cooker.

Serves 4–6
For the pastry
100g (3½oz) suet
200g (7oz) self-raising flour
pinch of salt
iced water

For the filling
900g (2lb) lean stewing or braising steak, cut into cubes
250g (9oz) beef kidneys, trimmed and cut into cubes
3 tbsp plain flour, seasoned with salt and pepper
50g (1¾oz) button mushrooms
1 tbsp Worcestershire sauce
dash of Tabasco
1 tbsp Chinese oyster sauce
a little beef stock or water
freshly ground black pepper

Preheat the slow cooker to high, and grease your pudding basin. Mix the suet, flour and salt in a bowl and, using a tablespoon at a time, slowly add enough iced water to bind. This can be done in a food processor, but don't overmix. Cover the pastry with cling film and chill for 20 minutes.

Keep about a quarter of the pastry back to make the lid, then roll out the other three quarters to a thickness of about 3mm (⅛in). Butter the pudding basin and line it with the rolled-out pastry, leaving about 3cm (1¼in) of pastry hanging over the top. Set aside.

Now make the filling by tossing the steak and beef kidneys in the seasoned flour. Mix the meat with the mushrooms and pile it all into the pastry-lined basin. Sprinkle with the Worcestershire sauce, Tabasco and Chinese oyster sauce. Pour in enough beef stock or water to fill two-thirds (or slightly more) of the dish. Season the pudding with plenty of pepper.

Roll out the remaining pastry to make a lid. Cover the pudding and fold the edges together to form a seal, pressing lightly.

Cover with greased greaseproof paper or foil, and lower into the slow cooker using a lifting strap (see page 155). Pour in enough water to come halfway up the sides of the basin. Put the lid on and cook on high for 6 to 8 hours.

Options

• Try using dried porcini mushrooms for added flavour. Soak them in water first, following the instructions on the packet, then add the soaking water to your crockpot.

Venison Stew with Walnuts and Prunes

This rich stew is perfect for winter weekend cooking. You can prepare it at your leisure, then leave it to cook while you venture out into the cold or relax in front of a blazing fire.

Serves 4–6
4 tbsp plain flour
salt and pepper
1¼kg (2¾lb) venison shoulder, off the bone, cut into small chunks
1 tbsp olive oil
50g (1¾oz) butter
2 medium carrots, sliced
2 medium onions, sliced
3 celery sticks, sliced
300ml (10fl oz) red wine
230g (8oz) pickled walnuts
100g (3½oz) dried prunes
400ml (14fl oz) vegetable or beef stock
4 sprigs of fresh thyme or ½ tsp dried
1 bay leaf

Preheat the slow cooker to high. In a large bowl, dredge the venison with flour seasoned liberally with salt and pepper.

In a large saucepan, heat the olive oil and the butter, then brown the meat. Remove from the pan and add the carrots, onions and celery. Cook for 2–3 minutes, scraping up any browned bits from the bottom of the pan as you cook. Place the vegetables in the bottom of the slow cooker, then put the venison on top. Pour over the red wine, then add the walnuts, prunes and stock. Stir in the thyme, add the bay leaf and cover. Cook on high for 30 minutes, then reduce the heat to low, cooking for 8 hours. The meat will be fork tender when it's ready.

Options

- Serve with mashed potatoes or mashed butter beans, or accompany with soft polenta and some greens. If desired, stir 2 tbsp Parmesan cheese into your soft polenta before serving, and top with toasted pine nuts.
- Any dried fruit will add substance and flavour to this fragrant stew. Why not stir in a handful each of dried, chopped apricots, dried sour cherries, dried cranberries and sultanas with the dried prunes?
- A pinch of cinnamon will warm the dish and create a festive flavour.

Chunky Rabbit and Apricot Stew

The sweet apricots are a delicious addition to the meaty rabbit. Serve with wild rice and broccoli, and, if desired, top with toasted walnuts.

Serves 4–6
1kg (2¼lb) rabbit pieces, skin removed; boneless is nice, but bones in will provide plenty of flavour
2 tbsp plain flour
30g (1oz) butter
1 medium onion, roughly chopped
2 medium carrots, roughly chopped
400g (14oz) tin chopped tomatoes
300ml (10fl oz) chicken stock
200g (7oz) dried apricots, roughly chopped
1 tsp dried thyme
salt and pepper to taste

Preheat the slow cooker to high. Dredge the rabbit pieces in the flour. Heat the butter in a saucepan and brown the rabbit on all sides. Transfer to the slow cooker and add the onions and carrots to the saucepan. Cook for 4 to 5 minutes, or until the onions are just slightly softened. Add the remaining ingredients to the saucepan, making sure you scrape the bottom of the pan as you stir, to deglaze.

Transfer everything to the slow cooker. Add a little water if the vegetables are not completely covered. Cook on low for 6 to 8 hours. Season to taste, and serve.

Poultry

Poultry is a great choice for slow-cooked meals, and by using the 'cheaper' cuts, such as legs and thighs (which actually impart much more flavour) you can save money too. Free-range, corn-fed and organic poultry is versatile, healthy and bursting with flavour, making it ideal for family meals or entertaining. Chicken, turkey, duck, goose and other fowl all fall under the poultry 'umbrella' and form the basis of a huge range of delicious meals that require little preparation. Remember that lighter poultry, such as chicken and turkey, does not need as much seasoning as the deeper-flavoured birds like pheasant and grouse.

Preparing poultry for slow cooking

It's easy to cook whole poultry in a slow cooker, and small birds can easily fit into an average-sized appliance. You can expect tender, moist results and a delicious, healthy meal. Bear in mind the following when using poultry in the slow cooker:

- Choose a bird that fits easily inside the slow cooker. The lid will need to fit firmly on top, and there should be at least a centimetre between the top of the bird and the lid.
- No liquid is required when roasting in the slow cooker; however, you can choose to add a little lemon juice or wine, for example, to impart some flavour.
- Onions, herbs, spices and even a lemon can be placed inside the chicken to give added flavour.
- Whole chickens should always be cooked on high, and will take between three and five hours, depending on size; however, portions can be cooked on high or low, depending upon how much time you have on your hands.
- Keep chicken on the bone if possible, as this provides the most flavour and also ensures that the meat doesn't cook too quickly. Added to soups and stews, you'll have little need for stock, as the bones will give flavour to the broth.

- Whole legs from large birds, such as turkey, will feed a crowd, and tend to be much cheaper than the crown or the breast.
- Whole duck should not be used at all in a slow cooker, as its shape makes it difficult to cook evenly, and its fat content can make a mess of your meal. Instead, use the slow cooker for smaller cuts, such as legs and breasts. Similarly, geese are large, fatty birds and are best prepared in the oven.

Chicken with Courgettes and Tarragon

Tarragon is the perfect herb to accompany chicken, giving this dish a deliciously fragrant flavour.

Serves 4–6
15g (½oz) butter
1 tbsp olive oil
1.4kg (3lb) whole chicken, giblets removed
salt and pepper
zest and juice of 1 lemon
1 tbsp dried tarragon
2 large courgettes, cut into chunks

Preheat the slow cooker to high. Heat the butter and oil in a large frying pan, and add the chicken, browning all sides. Transfer to the slow cooker and sprinkle with salt, pepper, lemon zest and juice and tarragon. Place the courgettes around the outside of the chicken.

Cover and cook on high for 3 to 4 hours. Once cooked, remove the chicken and courgettes from the slow cooker, cover and set aside to rest. Carve and serve.

Options
- This dish is wonderful served with mashed potatoes or rice, but it's also nice cold with a fresh green salad.
- To make a gravy, strain the juices into a small pan and thicken with a little cornflour mixed with water. Bring to the boil and stir until thickened. Serve alongside the chicken and courgettes.

Spanish Chicken Casserole

This is a straightforward but delicious meal. The succulent chicken is braised with Spanish sherry and onions until the meat literally falls off the bone into the richly flavoured sauce. Serve with wild rice and spring greens.

Serves 4–6
1 tbsp olive oil
1–1½kg (2¼lb–3lb 5oz) chicken thighs and drumsticks
4 medium onions, thinly sliced
2 green peppers, thinly sliced
6 cloves of garlic, thinly sliced
350ml (12fl oz) dry sherry
2 tbsp sherry vinegar
450ml (15fl oz) chicken stock
1 bay leaf
50g (1¾oz) toasted pine nuts
50g (1¾oz) sultanas

Preheat the slow cooker to high. In a large saucepan, heat the olive oil and brown the chicken until golden. Remove chicken from the oil and add the onions, peppers and garlic. When slightly softened, remove from the pan and place in the bottom of the slow cooker. Now, add a large wine glass of the sherry to the pan, and scrape up the bits from the bottom. Pour over the onions in the slow cooker and top with the browned chicken.

Add the remaining sherry, vinegar and stock and drop in the bay leaf. Cover and cook on high for 30 minutes, then reduce the heat and continue to cook for 4 to 6 hours on low. The chicken will be tender when cooked, and falling off the bone. Half an hour before the end of the cooking time, remove the lid and turn the heat up to high. Stir frequently to reduce the sauce slightly. Add the toasted pine nuts and sultanas, and serve.

Options

- Stir crème fraîche into any leftovers and use as an almost-instant sauce for pasta, or a topping for a baked potato.
- For a delicious, authentic Spanish flavour, omit the sultanas and pine nuts, and substitute 1 or 2 handfuls of large Spanish green olives stuffed with pimento, roughly chopped or added whole. Add about 30 minutes before serving so that they warm through.
- For a tangy flavour, sprinkle your casserole with the zest of half a lemon and a splash of sherry just before serving.

Braised Chicken with Mixed Mushrooms

Mixed mushrooms give a wonderful flavour to this hearty casserole, which is perfect for a cold winter's evening.

Serves 4–6
75g (2½oz) butter
3 tbsp olive oil
3 medium onions, finely sliced
2 tsp dried sage
2kg (4½lb) chicken thighs and drumsticks
12 cloves of garlic
300ml (10 fl oz) white wine
600ml (1 pint) chicken stock
450g (1lb) mixed mushrooms, such as chestnut, oyster, button and Portobello, sliced; dried mushrooms can also be used but don't need to be sliced
1 bay leaf
1 tsp dried thyme
3 tbsp Dijon mustard
salt and pepper

Preheat the slow cooker to high. In a large saucepan, heat the butter and oil. Add the onions and sage and cook until the onions are soft. Remove the onions and place in the bottom of the slow cooker. Use the oil to lightly brown the chicken, then place that in the slow cooker as well. Next, add the garlic cloves to the oil, and cook for 2 to 3 minutes. Remove and set aside. Pour over the white wine and use it to deglaze the pan – scraping up any bits that have become stuck. Tip into the slow cooker, and add the stock, mushrooms, bay leaf, thyme and mustard. Cover and cook for 30 minutes on high, then reduce the heat to low and continue to cook for 4 to 5 hours.

Season to taste, and serve immediately with mashed potatoes and some fresh green peas.

Options

- Rabbit can be used in place of chicken, for a meaty, gamey flavour. Use 2 x 1kg (2¼lb) rabbits, jointed.
- Whole baby onions can be added to the casserole, alongside the spices, for extra flavour and crunch. Make sure they are well peeled.
- If you like a creamier sauce, stir in 4 tbsp crème fraîche or double cream about 10 minutes before serving, and top with a little fresh sage, finely chopped or shredded.

Chermoula Chicken

Chermoula is a North African paste that – in its most basic form – is a combination of parsley, coriander and garlic. It's deliciously fragrant and fresh tasting and a perfect compliment to chicken and fish.

Serves 4–6
large bunch of fresh coriander, chopped
large bunch of flat-leaf parsley, chopped
3 large cloves of garlic
1 tsp ground cumin
2 tsp ground coriander
½ tsp cayenne pepper
salt and pepper
2 lemons, halved
2–3 tbsp olive oil
3 tbsp tomato purée
1½kg (3lb 5oz) chicken pieces
1 tbsp white wine vinegar
240ml (8fl oz) white wine

Preheat the slow cooker to high. Place the fresh coriander, parsley, garlic, cumin, ground coriander, cayenne, salt, pepper and the juice of both lemons in a food processor, and whiz until you have a rough paste. Stir in the oil and tomato purée and pulse a few more times.

Rub the chicken pieces with the paste, covering every surface. Pour the white wine vinegar and the wine into the bottom of the slow cooker, and throw in the lemon halves. Place the chicken pieces on top and cover. Cook on high for 45 minutes, reducing the heat to low and continuing to cook for another 4 to 5 hours.

Remove from the slow cooker with a slotted spoon, and pour over the cooking sauce. Serve with cous-cous or mashed butter beans and lightly steamed courgettes.

Lemon Chicken Tagine with Coriander

This fragrant Moroccan dish relies on preserved lemons for its flavour.
If you can't find preserved lemons, use the juice and zest of two lemons
instead.

Serves 4–6
2 tsp paprika
1 tsp ground cumin
1 tsp ground ginger
1 tsp turmeric
½ tsp cinnamon
¼ tsp freshly ground pepper
1 medium chicken, cut into 8 pieces
2 tbsp olive oil
3 cloves of garlic, minced
1 large onion, chopped
4 small preserved lemons, cut into slices
300ml (10fl oz) chicken stock
3 handfuls of green olives, pitted
2 handfuls of fresh coriander, chopped

Preheat the slow cooker to high. Mix the spices and rub into the outside
of the chicken pieces. Heat the olive oil in a large saucepan and brown
the chicken. Remove with a slotted spoon, then add the garlic and onion
to the pan, cooking until softened. Place in the bottom of the slow
cooker, with the chicken on top. Place the lemons around the chicken
and cover with stock. Cook on high for 45 minutes, then reduce the heat
and continue cooking on low for 4 to 5 hours.

An hour before serving, add the green olives and one handful of
fresh coriander. Cover and resume cooking.

When the chicken is falling off the bone, serve with the juices,
garnished with plenty of fresh coriander, on a bed of cous-cous.

Peanut Chicken Curry

This West African-inspired dish makes a delicious dinner-party dish, accompanied by basmati or fragrant Thai jasmine rice.

Serves: 4–6
1½kg (3lb 5oz) chicken pieces on the bone, skinless
4 tbsp flour
4 tbsp curry powder
2 tsp sea salt
½ tsp ground peppercorns
120ml (4fl oz) olive oil
2 tbsp fresh ginger, minced
2 tbsp garlic, minced
2 small red chilli peppers, seeded and minced
1 litre (1¾ pints) chicken stock
5 tbsp peanut butter
1 tsp ground coriander
8 spring onions, chopped
handful of finely chopped coriander, to garnish
handful of finely chopped mint, to garnish

Preheat the slow cooker to high. Rinse the chicken and pat it dry. Combine the flour, curry powder, salt and pepper in a large bowl, then add the chicken pieces. Using your hands, turn the chicken so that it is coated completely.

Heat the oil in a large saucepan and brown the chicken. Place in the bottom of the slow cooker, along with any scrapings from the pan. Add the ginger, garlic, chilli, stock and peanut butter and stir until combined. Cover and cook on high for 30 minutes, reducing the heat to low and cooking for a further 4 to 5 hours.

Just before serving, add the ground coriander and spring onions, and season to taste. Serve immediately with rice, and garnish each serving with a little fresh coriander and mint.

Options

- Instead of basmati or jasmine rice, make your own coconut rice in the microwave or a saucepan. Simply prepare your rice as usual, but cook for only half the time suggested on the packet. Drain and return to your saucepan or microwave bowl, and stir in a small tin of coconut milk. Continue cooking until the coconut milk has been absorbed and the rice is tender, adding a little extra water if required. The rice should be moist and slightly creamy, but not too saucy. Stir in a curry leaf or two when you add the coconut milk, for extra flavour. Coconut rice can be served with any curry dish.
- Sprinkle toasted peanuts on top for extra crunch.

Braised Pheasant with Sherry

These little birds cook beautifully in the slow cooker and, along with the rich sherry sauce, are perfect served with some fluffy mashed potatoes and a green salad.

Serves 4–6
For the pheasant
50g (1¾oz) butter
2 rashers streaky bacon, finely chopped
1 medium onion, finely chopped
2 celery sticks, thinly sliced
100g (3½oz) mixed mushrooms, thinly sliced
1 large pheasant (or 2 small)
salt and pepper to taste
½ tsp thyme

For the sauce
2 tbsp tomato purée
¼ tsp grated nutmeg
150ml (5fl oz) chicken stock
150ml (5fl oz) medium sherry
2 tsp cornflour
1 bay leaf

Preheat the slow cooker to high. Heat the butter in a large saucepan and add the bacon, onion and celery. Cook until the bacon is almost crispy. Stir in the mushrooms then, using a slotted spoon, transfer everything to the slow cooker.

Now add the pheasant to the pan, turning until brown on all sides. Transfer to the slow cooker and sprinkle with thyme. Blend together the tomato purée, nutmeg, chicken stock and sherry, and whisk in a little cornflour. Pour over the pheasant, along with the bay leaf.

Cook on high for 3 to 4 hours. Lift out the pheasant and set aside, keeping it warm. Take out the bay leaf and transfer the cooking juices to a small saucepan. Boil on a high heat for about 5 or 10 minutes, until the sauce thickens. Serve with the pheasant.

Options

- If you can't lay your hands on pheasant, try small chickens or poussin instead.
- Use the carcass of your pheasant to make a tasty soup. Simply place it in your slow cooker along with any remaining sherry sauce, a bouquet garni, 1 stalk of chopped celery, 1 peeled, chopped carrot, 2 medium potatoes, peeled and chopped, 1 tbsp sherry, 1 trimmed, sliced leek, a knob of butter and 1 litre boiling water. Simmer for 5 to 7 hours. You can either strain completely, and use the remaining liquid as a fragrant, rich stock, or lift out the vegetables and any usable pheasant meat with a slotted spoon, and put to one side, then strain the carcase and stir the vegetables and meat into the sauce. Continue cooking until the liquid reduces a little, seasoning to taste.

Poached Duck with Orange and Lime

The flavour combinations in this dish are outstanding, and the fruity citrus sauce complements the rich duck perfectly. Serve with fluffy rice, and some stir-fried greens.

Serves 4–6
1 large duck, cut into 8 pieces
5 tbsp olive oil
300ml (10fl oz) chicken stock
10 whole cloves
1 fresh hot chilli, whole
120ml (4fl oz) fresh orange juice
2 tbsp fresh lime juice
100g (3½oz) red bell pepper, finely chopped
¼ tsp salt
1 large orange, cut into wedges, to garnish

Preheat the slow cooker to high. Dry the duck completely with a tea towel and remove any loose skin and fat. In a large saucepan, heat the oil and brown the duck on all sides. Transfer to the slow cooker, then add the chicken stock, cloves and chilli. Cook for 45 minutes on high, then turn down the heat to low and continue cooking for another 2 hours.

At the end of this time, skim as much fat as possible from the surface and discard the cloves and chilli. Add the orange juice, lime juice, red peppers and salt. Continue cooking for another 2 to 3 hours, until the duck is tender and produces a clear liquid when pierced near to the bone.

Place the duck on a warmed serving plate and spoon over the sauce. Garnish with orange wedges.

Options
- Chicken or pheasant can be substituted for duck, as the citrus flavours complement both. Squeeze some extra lime over the poultry before serving, and garnish with a sprinkling of the zest.

Green Chicken Curry with Mango

A mild curry, that can be spiced up with extra chillies if you like it hot.

Serves 4–6
2 large red chillies, deseeded
grated zest and juice of 1 lime
2 lemongrass stalks, roughly chopped
5cm (2in) piece of fresh root ginger, peeled and sliced
4 garlic cloves, peeled
1 small onion, peeled and quartered
1 tsp shrimp paste
3 tbsp Thai fish sauce
1kg (2¼lb) chicken pieces
2 x 400ml (14fl oz) tins coconut milk
1 large mango, peeled and chopped into chunks
2 handfuls of fresh coriander

Preheat the slow cooker to high. Place the chillies, lime juice and zest, lemongrass, ginger, garlic, onion, shrimp paste and fish sauce in a food processor and blend to make a curry paste.

Place the chicken pieces in the slow cooker and pour over the coconut milk. Stir in the curry paste and cover. Cook on low for 6 to 8 hours. About 30 minutes before you wish to serve, stir in the mango chunks and a handful of fresh coriander.

Serve with Thai jasmine rice, and garnish with the remaining handful of fresh coriander.

Options
• This delicious dish can also be made with any white fish. Add in bite-size chunks for the last 30 minutes of cooking.

Sweet and Sour Chicken

This is a tangy dish with Oriental overtones, and it's perfect served with rice and stir-fried vegetables.

Serves 4–6
1 tbsp olive oil
10 chicken thighs, skin removed
1 medium onion, thinly sliced
1 green pepper, thinly sliced
1 celery stick, thinly sliced
2 tbsp cornflour
230g (8oz) tin pineapple chunks in juice, drained, chopped in half and juice reserved
4 tbsp cider vinegar
1 tbsp soy sauce
75g (2½oz) dark brown sugar
salt and pepper to taste

Preheat the slow cooker to high. Heat the oil in a large saucepan, and brown the chicken thighs in batches. Remove and place in the slow cooker. Add the onion, green pepper and celery to the pan and allow to soften then add to the slow cooker.

Mix together the cornflour with the pineapple juice and whisk until smooth. Stir in the cider vinegar, soy sauce and brown sugar, and add to the pan. Bring to the boil and, when slightly thickened, pour over the chicken. Cover and cook on low for 4 to 6 hours.

Options
- Stir in a handful of mangetout and baby sweetcorn about an hour before cooking for a 'one pot' meal.

Jambalaya

This traditional Creole dish has plenty of ingredients, but it couldn't be simpler to make. The flavour combinations are out of this world.

Serves 4–6
450g (1 lb) boneless, skinless chicken breasts, cut into 2½cm (1in) cubes
250g (9oz) chorizo sausage, cut into chunks
400g (14oz) tin chopped tomatoes
1 medium onion, chopped
1 green pepper, seeded and chopped
1 celery stick, chopped
240ml (8fl oz) chicken stock
2 tsp dried oregano
2 tsp Cajun or Creole seasoning
1 tsp hot chilli or pepper sauce
2 bay leaves
½ tsp dried thyme
250g (9oz) prawns, peeled and cooked
500ml (18fl oz) cooked white rice

In a preheated slow cooker, combine chicken, chorizo, tomatoes, onion, green pepper, celery and chicken stock. Stir in oregano, Cajun (or Creole) seasoning, hot sauce, bay leaves and thyme. Cover, and cook on low for 7 hours.

Stir in the prawns, cover and cook until heated through (about 5 minutes). Discard bay leaves and stir in the cooked rice. Cook until steaming hot and serve.

Options
• Any shellfish can be added to your Jambalaya – king prawns, mussels, clams – but make sure it is thoroughly cooked before serving.

Fish and Seafood

Many people are surprised to learn that fish can be successfully cooked in a slow cooker. The secret is to add it later on in the cooking process. You can, however, create dishes that involve leaving the fish and seafood in a little longer, and it will be as moist and flavourful as it would be if cooked in any other way. Both fish and shellfish easily take on the flavours of whatever they are cooked with, so go easy on the seasoning. One of the beauties of slow-cooking fish is the fact that the smell is trapped in the cooker, and your house will remain odour-free.

Baking and poaching fish in a slow cooker

Whole fish and steaks, such as tuna or swordfish, work particularly well when baked in a slow cooker, but you can adapt most recipes to ensure that your fish is beautifully flavoured while cooking. There are a few things, however, to bear in mind:

- The fish will need to fit into the slow cooker. It can be a good idea to line the bottom with foil and grease the foil with a little olive oil or butter, to prevent sticking. Dot the fish itself with butter or brush with olive oil too. If you wish, you can use a flavoured oil or a nut or seed oil, such as sesame, to provide more flavour.
- Cover and cook fish steaks for about 2 to 3 hours on low, or, if you are in a hurry, about 1 to 2 hours on high. If you are cooking a whole fish, you'll have a little longer to play with. Whole fish normally take about 3 to 4 hours on low heat, and about half that on high.
- Poaching fish provides a moist, fragrant result, in which the fish takes on the scent of whatever spices and herbs you use. This is one case where fresh herbs work well, as the cooking time is significantly shorter than it is for meat dishes. Simply grease the inside of the slow cooker, season your fish with herbs and spices, and perhaps the zest of a lemon or a lime, then pour enough liquid

into the slow cooker so that it reaches about halfway up the fish. Wine, fruit juices, cider, fish stock and even water all make good choices. Cover and cook on low for about 2 to 3 hours, and on high for about half that time. To make a sauce, remove the fish with a slotted spoon and keep warm. Transfer the cooking juices to a small saucepan and thicken with a little cornflour mixed with water. Bring to the boil and continue cooking, stirring frequently, until it reaches the desired consistency.

The best fish and seafood for slow cooking

When choosing fish for the slow cooker, select sturdy ones like sword-fish, salmon, halibut, cod, haddock and tuna. The fish should be cut into pieces of 2½cm (1in) or larger, then added during the last hour or so of cooking. To test whether or not the fish is cooked, flake it with a fork. If it's fully cooked, it should flake easily.

Shellfish toughen if overcooked, so the same timing principle holds true for shellfish, such as prawns and scallops. Stir them in for the last 15 to 60 minutes of cooking time, depending on the quantity and cooking temperature. If you are using frozen shellfish, make sure they are defrosted before being added to the slow cooker. Other varieties of shellfish, such as mussels and clams, are great for stews and are well suited to a white wine- or tomato-based sauce.

Delicate fish such as sole and flounder are not really compatible with slow cookers; they will often fall apart because they are so thin. Having said that, you can always place them in the slow cooker, in a foil packet that is open at the top, and cook them that way. They'll still take on the flavours of the liquid in which they are cooking and will be more likely to remain whole if they are tightly wrapped. After the fish has finished cooking, it should not be left to keep warm in the slow cooker, as this will cause it to dry out.

Salmon Risotto with Asparagus

It's easy to make a creamy, tasty risotto in the slow cooker. The secret is to check it frequently during the last 30 minutes, as slow cookers can vary enormously in cooking times. With slow-baked salmon and *al dente* asparagus, this risotto is a real summer treat.

Serves 4–6
450g (1lb) asparagus, cut into 2½cm (1in) chunks
75ml (2½fl oz) olive oil
2 shallots, peeled and chopped finely
250g (9oz) Arborio rice
75ml (2½fl oz) dry white wine
50g (1¾oz) butter
1 litre (1¾ pints) chicken stock
1 tsp salt
4–6 salmon steaks or fillets, any size
2 tbsp fresh basil, finely chopped
2 tsp lemon juice
salt and pepper to taste
75g (2½oz) freshly grated Parmesan cheese

Blanch the asparagus for about 2 minutes in boiling, salted water. Remove with a slotted spoon, and refresh in a bowl of ice-cold water. Drain and set aside.

In a saucepan, heat the oil and sauté the shallots until soft. Add the rice and stir until all the grains are coated. Add the wine and scrape up any bits from the bottom of the pan.

Next, grease the slow cooker with a little butter and leave the remainder of the butter at the bottom of the pot. Transfer the contents of the saucepan to the slow cooker and add the stock and salt. Cover and cook on high for about 60 minutes.

Next, pat the salmon dry and press on the fresh basil. Sprinkle with lemon juice, and season to taste with salt and pepper. Lay the salmon on top of the cooking risotto, and close the lid.

Continue cooking for another 30 to 45 minutes – checking halfway to see if the rice is *al dente*, all the liquid is absorbed, and the salmon is cooked through.

When it's ready, remove the salmon and put to one side. Stir in the asparagus and the Parmesan cheese. Break the salmon into neat chunks, and stir into the risotto. Serve immediately with lots of black pepper, and a fresh green salad.

Options
- Instead of asparagus and salmon, you could try fresh green beans and cod.

Lemon and Dill Salmon

This light, traditionally flavoured salmon dish is excellent served cold or warm. You can use salmon fillets or steaks, as you prefer.

Serves 4–6
50g (1¾oz) butter
1 spring onion, finely chopped
handful of fresh dill, finely chopped
salt and pepper to taste
zest and juice of 1 lemon
4–6 salmon steaks or fillets, any size
240ml (8fl oz) fish stock
60ml (2fl oz) white wine

Mix together the butter, onion, dill, salt and pepper and the zest and juice of the lemon. Use a little to grease the inside of the slow cooker, then smear the remainder over both sides of the fish fillets. Place in the slow cooker and add the stock and white wine. Cook for 1 to 2 hours on low.

Check the fish to make sure it is perfectly cooked, then serve with a green salad and some rice, drizzling the cooking liquid over before serving.

Options
• Serve your salmon cold on a bed of salad leaves, with a dressing of olive oil, lemon juice and chopped fresh dill.

Crème Fraîche Monkfish Cheeks

This French-inspired dish is a real treat, and can be confidently served at dinner parties. Although monkfish cheeks can be expensive, the rich, creamy sauce means that you can get away with serving fairly small portions.

Serves 4–6
6–10 monkfish cheeks
handful each of chives, chervil, dill, parsley and coriander, finely chopped
1 clove of garlic, crushed
50g (1¾oz) butter
180ml (6fl oz) fish stock, plus one fish stock cube
90ml (3fl oz) white wine
8 tbsp full-fat crème fraîche

Grease the inside of the slow cooker and lay the fish in the bottom. Cover with the herbs and garlic, and turn the fish so that they are coated. Dot with butter, and pour in the stock and the white wine. Crumble the fish stock cube over the top. Cook on low for 1 to 2 hours, checking about halfway. When cooked, remove the fish from the slow cooker and cover with aluminium foil.

Now, decant the cooking juices into a small saucepan, and reduce by about half. Stir in the crème fraîche. Pour over the fish, and serve with rice or sautéed potatoes and salad.

Options
• A light sherry can be used instead of white wine for an even richer flavour.

Trout with Apple and Almond Stuffing

This is a delicious, quick recipe that is bursting with flavour.

Serves 4–6
3–4 whole trout, cleaned
2 tbsp butter
2 green apples, peeled, cored and roughly chopped
1 small onion, finely chopped
½ red pepper, finely chopped
½ green pepper, finely chopped
1 celery stick, finely chopped
600ml (1 pint) fish stock
250g (9oz) breadcrumbs
1 tbsp fresh rosemary
50g (1¾oz) toasted, flaked almonds
salt and pepper to taste

Rinse trout and pat dry. Grease the slow cooker with a little butter.

In a saucepan, melt the remaining butter and gently sauté the apples, onion, peppers and celery until very soft (about 10 minutes). Add about 150ml (5fl oz) fish stock, and the breadcrumbs and rosemary. Stir until the stock is absorbed, adding a little more if the mixture is too dry. Stir in the almonds and season to taste. Spoon the mixture inside the trout.

Place the trout cut-side up in the slow cooker, in two layers if necessary. Pour the remaining stock around. Cook for 2 to 3 hours on low heat, checking part of the way through to ensure the fish does not overcook.

Serve with a fresh green salad and some lightly sautéed potatoes.

Options
- Try adding a handful of finely chopped sultanas and dried apricots to your stuffing in the place of the peppers.

Spicy Mediterranean Prawns

These robust prawns are perfect served with cous-cous or even a thin pasta, such as linguine, to create a light, but very tasty meal.

Serves 4–6
2 tsp paprika
6 spring onions, finely chopped
100g (3½oz) green olives stuffed with pimentos, sliced
100g (3½oz) pickled green chillies, finely chopped (jalapenos will do)
handful of fresh parsley, chopped
3 tbsp olive oil
juice of 1 lime
salt and pepper to taste
400g (14oz) prawns, raw, peeled and deveined
150ml (5fl oz) fish stock
60ml (2fl oz) white wine

Grease the slow cooker. Blend the first eight ingredients into a paste in a food processor. Coat the prawns in the mixture and place them in the bottom of the slow cooker. Add the fish stock and white wine. Cover and cook on low for about 30 to 60 minutes, or a little longer if the prawns are big.

Give the prawns a stir to blend together the sauce, then ladle on to cous-cous or pasta. Serve with a spinach salad.

Options
- If you are using pre-cooked prawns, add them 15 minutes before serving. Make sure frozen prawns are fully defrosted first.

Yellow Prawn Curry

This is a tasty, very lightly spiced curry that goes nicely with meaty prawns.

Serves 4–6
6 tbsp fresh ginger, grated
2 onions, chopped
2 cloves of garlic, minced
1 tbsp sesame oil
3 tbsp yellow curry paste
2 lemongrass stalks, bruised
1 tsp fish sauce
1 tbsp hot chilli sauce
1 tbsp butter
2 x 400ml (14fl oz) tins coconut milk
3 large carrots, chopped
4 large white potatoes, peeled and chopped
3 tsp dried coriander leaves
700ml (1¼ pints) vegetable stock
250g (9oz) prawns, raw, peeled and deveined
large bunch of coriander, chopped

In a small saucepan, sauté the ginger, onion and garlic in the sesame oil for 10 minutes. Tip into the slow cooker and add all of the remaining ingredients apart from the prawns and the fresh coriander. Cook on low for 7 to 8 hours.

About 30 minutes from the end of cooking time, stir in the prawns and half of the coriander. Cook until the prawns are firm and a good pink colour.

Serve on a bed of rice with chopped, fresh coriander scattered on top.

Options

- Like your curry a little spicier? Finely chop a small, hot red chilli and add to the ginger, onion and garlic mixture.
- You can substitute bite-size pieces of chicken for the prawns, but count on adding about 2 hours to the cooking process.
- You can add any vegetables to this curry, such as baby corn, baby aubergines, green beans, mangetout or sugar snap peas; simply ensure that they are all cut to roughly the same size, and that green vegetables and previously frozen vegetables are added later on in the cooking time.
- If desired, omit the prawns or other meat entirely, and serve as a vegetarian option or side dish for a Thai feast. This curry tastes delicious with coconut rice (see page 83) or fragrant, sticky Thai rice.

Spanish Paella

A traditional Spanish paella may not be an obvious choice for the slow cooker, but the end result is well worth the effort. There is a lot of shellfish in this recipe, but if you have problems laying your hands on it, simply add more prawns or chunks of firm, white fish, such as cod or haddock.

Serves 4–6
2 tbsp olive oil
450g (1lb) chorizo sausage, cut into chunks
1 green pepper, chopped
1 medium red onion, chopped
4 cloves of garlic, minced
½ teaspoon crushed red pepper flakes
450g (1lb) long-grain white rice
600ml (1 pint) fish stock
240ml (8fl oz) tomato juice
120ml (4fl oz) water
240ml (8fl oz) dry white wine
¼ tsp ground turmeric
¼ tsp freshly ground black pepper
1 tsp salt
½ tsp dried basil
400g (14oz) tin artichoke hearts, drained
12 small clams or mussels in the shell, rinsed and scrubbed
450g (1lb) medium-sized prawns, raw, peeled and deveined
450g (1lb) cooked crab legs, in the shell, cracked

In a large saucepan, heat the olive oil and brown the chorizo sausage for about 10 minutes. Combine all of the remaining ingredients, apart from the clams, prawns and crab legs, in the slow cooker, and stir well to blend. Turn the heat to high, cover and cook for 4 to 6 hours, stirring twice during the cooking process.

About 30 minutes from the end of cooking time, add the clams, prawns and crab legs and cover again. Continue cooking until the clams open (about 20 to 30 minutes). Discard any that do not open.

Give the paella one final stir and serve piping hot in large, shallow bowls, or decant on to a large platter with the shellfish arranged on top.

Options

- Any fish or shellfish can be used in paella – choose the freshest you can find, and take care to clean them carefully.
- Sprinkle your paella with 2 tsp freshly grated lemon zest along with 2 tsp each of finely chopped fresh parsley and fresh basil, for a fragrant finishing touch.
- You can also finely chop a handful of green Spanish olives, stuffed with pimento, and sprinkle over the paella before serving.

Plaice, Potato and Spinach Bake

This is comfort food of the very highest order, and ideal for a family supper or an informal dinner with friends. You can create as many layers as you wish, but you'll have to serve straight from the slow cooker pot to avoid having to dismantle your creation.

Serves 4–6
75g (2½oz) butter
1 tbsp olive oil
2 large leeks, washed, trimmed and finely sliced
450g (1lb) spinach, washed and thick stems removed
pinch of freshly grated nutmeg
salt and pepper
150ml (5fl oz) milk
270ml (9fl oz) double cream
3 cloves of garlic, crushed
75g (3oz) Parmesan cheese
750g (1lb 10oz) white potatoes, scrubbed and very thinly sliced
2 large plaice, filleted and skinned, cut into thin slices
juice of 1 lemon

Grease the inside of the slow cooker with a little butter. Heat the oil and remaining butter in a large saucepan and cook the leeks until soft. Add the spinach to the pan and stir for a few minutes. Turn off the heat and cover; leave for about 5 minutes, or until the spinach has wilted. Add the nutmeg and salt and pepper. Drain the spinach and leek mixture, reserving the liquid, and put to one side.

Next, add the milk, cream and garlic, along with the reserved liquid from the spinach and leeks, to the same saucepan and bring to the boil. Simmer for a few minutes, then grate in the Parmesan cheese. Take off the heat and set aside.

Place a layer of potatoes in the slow cooker, and top with some spinach and leek, then a layer of thinly sliced fish. Pour a little lemon juice over the fish, then cover with a little of the cheesy cream. Continue layering in this way, finishing with the cheesy cream. Grate on a little more Parmesan and adjust seasoning to taste. Place the lid on the slow cooker and cook on high for 5 to 8 hours. When it's done, the potatoes will be tender, and the whole bake will be bubbling.

If your pot is ovenproof, pop it under the grill for a few minutes to brown the top. Serve immediately.

Options

- Any white fish can be used instead of plaice, and spring onions or shallots make a good substitute for leeks.

Rich Shellfish Stew

There may be a lot of ingredients involved, but this recipe is easy to prepare and results in a fantastically tasty stew with intense flavours. The
large quantity of shellfish can make it an expensive dish, but you can
save it for occasions where you feel like making something special.

Serves 4–6
450g (1lb) mussels, cleaned and bearded (keep in ice-cold water until
required)
450g (1lb) monkfish, cut into 2½cm (1in) chunks
2 tbsp plain flour
2 tsp cayenne pepper
50g (1¾oz) butter
2 tbsp olive oil
200ml (7fl oz) white wine
3 cloves of garlic, crushed
4 large shallots, peeled and minced
300g (10½oz) scallops, shelled
450g (1lb) prawns, raw, peeled and deveined
100g (3½oz) baby leaf spinach
90ml (3fl oz) evaporated milk
270ml (9fl oz) fish stock
salt and pepper

Grease the inside of the slow cooker. Discard any mussels that don't
close when tapped. Toss the monkfish chunks in a mixture of the plain
flour and cayenne pepper until well coated.

Heat the butter and olive oil in a saucepan and gently brown the
monkfish. Remove from the pan and place in the bottom of the slow
cooker.

Pour the white wine into the saucepan to deglaze it then pour over the fish. Mix together the garlic and the shallots, then sprinkle over the fish and wine mixture. Next, place the scallops, prawns and mussels on top of the fish. Stir in the spinach, then the evaporated milk and the fish stock. Season to taste and cover. Cook on low heat for 2 to 3 hours, stirring occasionally.

When the seafood is plump and moist and the fish is cooked, serve piping hot in big bowls, with some crusty bread alongside.

Options

- Stir in some crème fraîche or even a small tub of cream cheese to create a delicious sauce for pasta or a filling for baked potatoes.
- For instructions on how to make your own fish stock, see page 47.

Haddock Florentine with Summer Vegetables

The rich cheese sauce coats the spinach, fish and summer vegetables, creating a delightfully tasty dish. Serve with plenty of crusty bread for mopping up the sauce.

Serves 4–6
200g (7oz) asparagus spears
100g (3½oz) freshly shelled peas
2 small courgettes, thickly sliced
250g (9oz) frozen spinach, thawed and drained
freshly grated nutmeg
salt and freshly ground pepper
4–6 skinless white haddock fillets
30g (1oz) butter
1 tbsp cornflour
300ml (10fl oz) milk
150g (5½oz) mature Cheddar cheese, grated
3 tomatoes, sliced

Grease the inside of the slow cooker. Blanch the asparagus, peas and courgette slices in boiling, salted water for 2 minutes, then refresh in a bowl of ice-cold water. Drain and place in the slow cooker with the spinach. Stir together and add a good grating of nutmeg and a little salt and pepper.

Place the haddock fillets on top of the vegetables, and season again.

In a small saucepan, melt the butter and stir in the cornflour. Stir until bubbling, then add the milk, simmering gently until thick. Season and stir in three-quarters of the cheese. Pour the cheese sauce over the fish and vegetables, making sure that it is completely covered. Now arrange the tomato slices around the edge of the pot. Cover and cook on low for 2 to 3 hours.

When the cooking time has finished, sprinkle with the remaining cheese and cover until melted or, if your pot is ovenproof, place under the grill until the cheese is golden brown and bubbling. Serve immediately.

Options

- A rich blue cheese such as Gorgonzola or St Azur can be used in the sauce instead of Cheddar.
- To make your meal more substantial, thinly slice some waxy, peeled potatoes and trimmed leeks, and layer in the bottom of the slow cooker, brushing each layer with a little melted butter and a sprinkling of salt, pepper and dried tarragon. Put the lid on your slow cooker and cook for 2 to 3 hours on high. Open, and continue with the recipe above, adding the blanched vegetables and cheese sauce directly on top of the potatoes and leeks. To serve, ladle out the haddock and vegetables, and then slice the layered potatoes and serve alongside.

Tuna Casserole Niçoise

This pasta dish is a delicious twist on the classic American tuna casserole and the French tuna salad. You can use tinned white tuna or lightly grilled tuna steaks – whichever suits your budget and your time.

Serves 4–6
120ml (4fl oz) olive oil
4 roasted red peppers in oil, drained and sliced
200g (7oz) black olives, pitted and chopped
200g (7oz) fresh green beans, or frozen and defrosted
2 cloves of garlic, minced
2 tsp dried oregano
2 tsp dried basil
400g (14oz) tin chopped tomatoes
salt and pepper
200g (7oz) feta cheese, crumbled
200g (7oz) penne
2 tuna steaks, lightly grilled and cut into chunks (or 2 x 185g/6½oz tins tuna in brine, drained)

Grease the slow cooker with a little of the olive oil. In the pot mix together the red peppers, olives, green beans, olive oil, garlic, oregano, basil, chopped tomatoes, salt, pepper and half of the feta cheese. Place the lid on the pot and cook for 2 to 3 hours on low.

Next, cook the penne in boiling water for about 7 minutes, then stir the partially cooked pasta into the sauce, along with the tuna. Cover with the remaining crumbled feta, and replace the lid. Cook for another 30 to 60 minutes. Serve immediately with a fresh green salad.

Options
- Top with toasted pine nuts for extra texture and flavour.

Vegetables

All vegetables can be cooked successfully in a slow cooker, and still maintain their crispness and vibrant colours. Some vegetables take longer than others to cook, meaning that you may need to open your pot to make additions as you go, but in most cases, you can create delicious recipes from vegetables that need similar cooking times.

Vegetables are naturally high in water, so you won't need to add much cooking liquid to the slow cooker. And while it is possible to dry roast vegetables, they'll always be softer than the oven-cooked varieties.

Slow cooking vegetables is a great way to bring out their natural flavour, leaving you with tender, juicy produce that is neither over-cooked nor tasteless. Vegetables are a vital component of virtually all slow cooker recipes, and you can create delicious meat-free dishes, making it a must for vegetarians.

Cooking vegetables in a slow cooker

Perhaps the most commonly used vegetable in all slow-cooked dishes is the onion. There are many varieties, but all respond best to being soft-ened before being added to a dish. If you are pressed for time, they can certainly go in raw, but they will never impart the same sweet, creamy flavour that lightly cooked onions do. Other members of the onion family include leeks, chives, spring onions, shallots and garlic, and all can be used successfully in the slow cooker, with or without pre-cook-ing. It's worth noting that onions become less pungent while slow-cooking, so you'll find that many recipes add more than you might expect, to give the dish the required punch.

Peppers are also commonly used for flavour and colour. Red and yel-low peppers are the best, as they become sweet and robustly flavoured when cooked. Green peppers can become bitter, so add these towards the end of your cooking time, and keep the pieces small.

Some of the softer, more delicate vegetables, such as mushrooms, tomatoes and courgettes will need to be added in the last hour or so of cooking to ensure that they cook well and do not disintegrate.

Dried mushrooms and tomato paste can, however, be added from the outset.

Root vegetables are a staple in many slow-cooked dishes and tend to take the longest time to cook. Surprisingly, perhaps, they take longer than meat to cook through. It's a good idea always to cut them into small pieces, preferably fairly uniformly sized, and place them at the bottom of the slow cooker.

Squash and pumpkin make delicious additions to many dishes, and hold their taste and texture despite long periods of cooking. They are moisture-rich, so don't be tempted to add a lot of liquid when cooking them.

Broccoli, cauliflower and cabbage work well in slow cookers, and can become meltingly tender if they are cooked in a little liquid. Leafy vegetables, such as spinach and kale, should be added later on in the cooking time, to ensure that they retain their colour, flavour and texture.

Don't hesitate to use frozen vegetables, which can make the process of slow cooking that much easier. Defrost and drain them before adding to your pot, as they can lower the temperature substantially if frozen, bringing the cooking process to a resounding halt.

Tinned vegetables should be drained prior to cooking and added later in the cooking time. The same goes for tinned pulses, such as chickpeas and cannellini beans, which need far less cooking than their dried, soaked counterparts.

Don't be put off by unusual vegetables, either. You can use fennel, pak choi, aubergines, sweet potatoes, Jerusalem artichokes, runner beans, baby sweetcorn and mangetout – virtually anything that appears on the supermarket shelves or at your local farmer's market. You may need to experiment a bit to get the timing right, but look for recipes with similar vegetables and use them as a guide.

Finally, potatoes can be cooked in any variety of ways, including baked: simply wrap them in foil and place them on top of anything else you are cooking. They'll be piping hot and ready to eat in 6 to 10 hours – and, with a bit of luck, their topping will be ready alongside.

Ratatouille

This classic French dish is about as easy at it gets, and the vegetables cook brilliantly in the rich tomato sauce. Use fresh, crisp vegetables if you can find them, and serve with a good chunk of fresh French bread and a little cheese.

Serves 4–6
2 large aubergines, chopped into chunks
2 large courgettes, chopped into chunks
2 red peppers, deseeded and chopped into chunks
1 yellow pepper, deseeded and chopped into chunks
1 large Spanish onion, peeled and chopped into chunks
2 x 400g (14oz) tins chopped tomatoes
1 tbsp tomato paste
4 cloves of garlic, minced
1 tsp sugar
1 tsp sea salt
2 tsp dried basil
2 tsp dried oregano
1 tsp dried thyme
90ml (3fl oz) red wine
freshly ground black pepper
60ml (2fl oz) olive oil

Simply stir together all of these ingredients, except for the oil, until thoroughly mixed. You can do this in the pot of the slow cooker. Drizzle with olive oil, and pop on the lid. Cook on low heat for 7 to 9 hours, then simply serve!

Options
- An hour before the end of cooking, top with grated mozzarella cheese, which will melt down into the stew for a stringy treat!

Lentils with Walnuts and Sherry

This is a wonderful side dish, served just warm or even cold, alongside fish, poultry or meat dishes.

Serves 4–6
450g (1lb) green or puy lentils, rinsed
700ml (1¼ pints) chicken stock
120ml (4fl oz) sherry
salt and pepper
3 tbsp sherry vinegar
6 tbsp olive oil
2 handfuls of fresh chives, chopped
100g (3½oz) toasted walnuts

Place the lentils, stock, sherry and salt and pepper in the slow cooker and mix thoroughly. Cover and cook on low for 5 to 6 hours, or until lentils are tender. Stir in the vinegar, olive oil and chives, and cook for a further 30 to 40 minutes. Add the toasted walnuts and allow to cool slightly before serving.

Options
• Top with grilled goat's cheese roundels for a perfect starter or light main course.

Braised Fennel

This makes a lovely side dish or it can be eaten hot or cold on its own. The aniseed flavour mellows beautifully while cooking, and very few ingredients are needed to create perfection!

Serves 4–6
2 small fennel bulbs per person, bottoms chopped off
80ml (3fl oz) olive oil
juice of 1 lemon
1 tsp sea salt
freshly ground black pepper

Grease the bottom of the slow cooker with a little olive oil and place the fennel bulbs upright inside it. Drizzle with olive oil and lemon juice and sprinkle with sea salt and pepper. Cover and cook on low for 8 to 10 hours, until the fennel is soft, but still holding its shape.

Options
• Try substituting orange juice and zest in place of lemon.

Thai Red Vegetable Curry

You can make this delicious, crunchy curry as spicy as you wish – just use a little more curry paste to give it more kick! Any vegetables can be used, but you'll need to gauge the cooking time to ensure that they are all equally cooked.

Serves 4–6
1 tbsp vegetable oil
1 medium onion, finely chopped
½ small butternut squash, cut into 2.5cm (1in) cubes
½ head of cauliflower, cut into florets
4 baby aubergines, cut into chunks
2 courgettes, cut into chunks
200g (7oz) tin water chestnuts, drained
200g (7oz) baby corn
200g (7oz) mangetout
1 red pepper, thinly sliced
400ml (14fl oz) tin coconut milk
1–2 tbsp red curry paste
2 tsp cornflour
juice of ½ lime
½ tsp fish sauce
fresh coriander or Thai basil, to garnish

Heat the oil in a large saucepan and add the onion. Fry for 2 to 3 minutes. Tip into the bottom of the slow cooker and top with the remaining vegetables. Next, mix the coconut milk with the red curry paste, and pour over the vegetables. Cook on low for 6 to 8 hours. About 30 minutes before the end of cooking time, mix together the cornflour, lime juice and fish sauce until smooth. Stir into the curry, cover and continue cooking. Sprinkle with coriander or Thai basil, and serve immediately with jasmine rice.

Options

- This fragrant red curry is delicious served with coconut rice (see page 83).
- For a meaty twist, thinly slice about 400g (14oz) hearty braising beef and gently toss in cornflour seasoned with salt, pepper and a pinch of dried coriander. Stir into the saucepan with the onion. Continue with the recipe, cooking until the curry is fragrant and the meat is tender.
- If you want something fishy with your curry, stir in some pre-cooked prawns about 15 minutes before serving.

Butternut Squash Risotto with Feta and Mint

This fragrant, light risotto is delicious year round, and perfect served with a crisp green salad.

Serves 4–6
70ml (2½fl oz) olive oil
3 back bacon rashers, sliced
2 leeks, washed, trimmed and thinly sliced
250g (9oz) Arborio risotto rice
70ml (2½fl oz) dry white wine
50g (1¾oz) butter
1 litre (1¾ pints) chicken stock
½ large butternut squash, cut into 2.5cm (1in) chunks
75g (2½oz) freshly grated Parmesan cheese
3 tbsp fresh mint, chopped
125g (5oz) feta cheese
salt and pepper, to taste

In a saucepan, heat the oil and sauté the bacon until starting to brown. Stir in the leeks and cook until softened. Add the rice and stir until all of the grains are coated. Add the wine and scrape up any bits from the bottom of the pan.

Next, grease the slow cooker with the butter, and leave the remainder at the bottom of the pot. Transfer the contents of the saucepan to the slow cooker, and add the stock. Stir in the butternut squash. Cover and cook on high for about 90 minutes. Check that the rice is al dente, and all the liquid is absorbed. Cover and cook for another 15 minutes if required. When it's done, stir in the Parmesan cheese and fresh mint. Crumble over the feta cheese, season to taste, and serve immediately.

Options
- Instead of mint, try fresh basil instead.
- Use pumpkin in the place of the butternut squash, or even peas (but they will need less cooking).

Creamy Leek and Chicory Casserole

This casserole is rich and warm, and takes full advantage of the delicious flavours of the leeks and the chicory. It's a great supper on its own, but also works well as a side dish for meat or fish.

Serves 4–6
50g (1¾oz) butter
100g (3½oz) smoked streaky bacon, cut into small pieces
3 large leeks, washed, trimmed and sliced
4 heads of chicory, cut into quarters and trimmed
50g (1¾oz) plain flour
600ml (1 pint) whole milk
150g (5½oz) mature Cheddar cheese, grated
salt and pepper

Heat half of the butter in a saucepan and brown the bacon for a few minutes. Add the sliced leeks and stir for a minute or two. Place the chicory in a pot of boiling water and cook for 3 to 4 minutes.

Add the remaining butter to the leeks, then stir in the flour. Cook for a few minutes, then add the milk. Simmer until the sauce is smooth and thick. Stir in the grated cheese and season with salt and pepper.

Butter the inside of the slow cooker and spread half the leeks on the bottom. Cover with all of the chicory, then with the rest of the leeks. Scatter with the remaining cheese and put on the lid. Cook on low for 5 to 6 hours.

If the slow cooker is ovenproof, pop it under the grill at the end of the cooking time for just a few minutes, to get a nice golden-brown topping. Serve piping hot.

Options
- Vegetarians can omit the bacon but add a tablespoon of vegetable or vegan stock powder to the sauce to enhance the flavour.

Braised Summer Vegetables with Pancetta and Sherry

This dish is rather like a soup, but with an intense flavour and a rustic feel. The sherry and the pancetta draw out the flavours of the summer vegetables, which are in season for such a short time that it's a shame not to use them whenever possible

Serves 4–6
olive oil
200g (7oz) sliced pancetta
1 medium onion, peeled and finely chopped
2 heads of roasted garlic (see opposite)
2 tbsp sherry vinegar
450g (1lb) new potatoes, cut into slices
300g (10½oz) baby carrots, scraped clean
450ml (15fl oz) vegetable stock
150ml (5fl oz) dry sherry
250g (9oz) shelled fresh peas
450g (1lb) broad beans, shelled
2 sprigs of fresh mint
small handful of fresh parsley
salt and pepper

Splash a good glug of olive oil in a saucepan and cook the pancetta until crisp. Remove from the pan, and set aside. Next, sweat the onion in the hot oil. When the onion is soft, squeeze the garlic heads from their roasted skins and stir into the onions. Add the sherry vinegar and bring to the boil.

Tip the onion mixture into the slow cooker and add the potatoes, carrots, stock and sherry. Cover and cook on low for 3 to 4 hours, then stir in the peas and broad beans. Continue cooking for another 60 to 90 minutes, then stir in the mint, parsley, salt, pepper and the pancetta. Cook for about 20 minutes more, until the pancetta is warmed through, and serve in bowls with chunks of crusty brown bread, or even on a bed of rice.

Options

- Any fresh summer herbs will add flavour to this sumptuous dish. Why not try tarragon and chervil, or some fresh chives and lemon thyme? Similarly, anything goes in the vegetables department: fresh, sliced crunchy lettuce, baby corn, spinach, mangetout and tender celery hearts make a delicious addition.

- Roasted garlic is available in most supermarkets, but if it's hard to find, you can make it yourself. Slice the top and bottom from a whole head of garlic, but leave the skins on. Drizzle with olive oil and roast at 200°C (400°F) for 30 to 35 minutes, until the cloves are soft when pressed. Separate before use.

Tomato Baked Eggs

This is a simple recipe that can be served for breakfast, brunch, lunch or even a light evening meal. The consistency of the slow-cooked eggs may be unfamiliar, but they are rich, gloopy and deeply satisfying when cooked in this way.

Serves 4–6
900g (2lb) ripe vine tomatoes, thickly sliced
salt and pepper
2 tbsp chopped parsley
2 tbsp chopped chives
3 cloves of garlic, thinly sliced
3 tbsp olive oil
4–6 large eggs
toasted ciabatta, to serve

Lightly oil the inside of the slow cooker and spread the sliced tomatoes over the bottom. If you need to create more than one layer, season between the layers with salt, pepper and a pinch each of parsley and chives. Sprinkle the garlic over the tomatoes, drizzle with olive oil and season again. Place the lid on the slow cooker and roast the tomatoes on high for 3 to 4 hours, or until glistening.

Make gaps between the tomato slices, and break an egg into each gap. Cover again and continue cooking for another 60 minutes, or until the eggs are set to your liking. Scatter with the remaining herbs, and serve piping hot with thick slices of ciabatta.

Options
• Serve on toasted brioche instead of ciabatta. The eggs are also delicious on a bed of lightly steamed or roasted asparagus.

Saag Paneer

This scrumptious Indian side dish has to be my favourite. Its rich flavours combine with the creamy cheese to produce a perfect accompaniment to any Indian dish, but it can also be eaten on its own as a satisfying supper.

Serves 4–6
1 large onion, finely chopped
6 cloves of garlic, peeled and chopped
30g (1oz) fresh ginger, grated
450g (1lb) frozen spinach, defrosted and drained
240ml (8fl oz) plain yoghurt
120ml (4fl oz) buttermilk
2 tsp red chilli powder
2 tsp garam masala
240ml (8fl oz) single cream
200g (7oz) paneer cheese, cut into bite-sized chunks

Blend the onion, garlic and ginger into a fine paste in a food processor.

In the slow cooker, combine the paste, spinach, yoghurt, buttermilk, chilli powder and garam masala. Cover and cook on low for 3 to 4 hours. Open the pot, stir and add the cream. Replace the lid and cook for another 60 minutes. Stir in the paneer, cover and cook for a further 30 minutes. Season to taste and serve.

Options
• If you can't find paneer cheese, a firm feta will do instead.

Cheesy Vegetable Hot Pot

This is perfect comfort food and ideal for serving a vegetarian crowd!
Use any selection of vegetables you have to hand.

Serves 4–6
2 tbsp butter
3 leeks, washed, trimmed and roughly chopped
½ small Savoy cabbage, shredded
10–12 chestnut mushrooms, sliced
3 Jerusalem artichokes, peeled and cut into chunks
1 small courgette, cut into chunks
1 yellow pepper, thickly sliced
1 tsp dried thyme
salt and pepper, to taste
4 tbsp crème fraîche
5 medium white potatoes, peeled and thinly sliced
2 tbsp butter
1 small Camembert or other rinded soft cheese, sliced with the rind on
1 tbsp fresh thyme, to garnish

Melt the butter in a saucepan, add the leeks and cook until softened
(about 8 minutes). Tip into the slow cooker, then stir in the cabbage,
mushrooms, Jerusalem artichokes, courgette and yellow pepper.
Sprinkle with thyme and salt and pepper, then mix in the crème fraîche.
Lay the potato slices over the vegetables, pressing them down, then dot
with butter. Cover with the cheese, and place the lid on your slow
cooker. Cook for 6 to 8 hours on low. Sprinkle with fresh thyme leaves,
and serve in bowls, immediately.

Options
•   If you prefer a 'golden' crust, place your hot pot under the grill for
    a few minutes before serving.

Lightly Spiced Dahl

This is a healthy, hearty meal on its own, served with poppadoms or naan bread. You can also halve the quantities for a tasty side dish.

Serves 4–6
2 tbsp butter
1 large onion, finely chopped
2 cloves of garlic, crushed
300g (10½oz) red lentils, rinsed well
5cm (2in) fresh ginger, grated
2 bay leaves
1 cinnamon stick
2 tsp turmeric
1 tsp cumin
½ tsp garam masala
½ tsp chilli flakes
2 tbsp lemon juice
salt and pepper, to taste
3 tbsp fresh coriander, chopped

Melt the butter in a large saucepan, add the onion and garlic and cook until softened (about 8 to 10 minutes). Tip into the bottom of the slow cooker, then stir in the lentils, ginger, bay leaves, cinnamon stick, turmeric, cumin, garam masala and chilli flakes, plus 700ml (1¼ pints) water. Cover and cook on low for 6 to 8 hours.

About 30 minutes before serving, stir in the lemon juice and season to taste. Cover and continue cooking. Sprinkle with fresh coriander and serve immediately.

Options
· Serve cool as a delicious dip with toasted pitta bread.

Slow Cooker Mashed Potatoes

This flavourful mash is beautifully simple. Just toss your potatoes in the slow cooker in the morning, and they'll be ready to mash in time for dinner.

Serves 4–6
2.5kg (5½lb) Charlotte potatoes, washed and cut into large chunks
270ml (9fl oz) water
1 tbsp salt
ground black pepper, to taste
125g (4½oz) salted butter, cut into chunks
350ml (12fl oz) milk, warmed

Place the potatoes, water, salt, pepper and butter into a slow cooker. Toss potatoes to coat. Cover and cook on low for 6 to 8 hours. Remove lid, mash potatoes (in the slow cooker), add the warmed milk and whip to desired consistency. Turn the slow cooker to warm setting until your main course is ready.

Options
• Stir in some grated, mature Cheddar cheese and grated red onion after mashing.

Vegetarian Chilli

This spicy chilli is piled high with chunky vegetables. Serve with soured cream and grated cheese, if desired, and with a green salad and/or garlic bread.

Serves 4–6
2 x 400g (14oz) tins whole plum tomatoes
400g (14oz) tin chickpeas, drained
2 courgettes, thickly sliced
1 onion, chopped
2 carrots, sliced
2 celery sticks, sliced
1 red pepper, coarsely chopped
1 yellow pepper, coarsely chopped
1 medium aubergine, cut into 2.5cm/1in chunks
1 tsp mild chilli powder
1 green chilli, seeded and chopped
2 cloves of garlic, minced
1 tbsp dried oregano
2 tsp ground cumin
salt and pepper, to taste

Place all of the ingredients in the slow cooker. Cover and cook on low for 6 to 8 hours (or, if you are in a rush, go for 3 to 4 hours on high). It's as simple as that!

Potatoes Dauphinois

This recipe hails from the Dauphine, a region of France known for its spectacular mountains, verdant forests and rich pasturelands, which lies between Savoy and Provence. It's the ideal side dish for meat or poultry.

Serves 4–6
75g (2½oz) salted butter, plus extra for greasing, cut into pieces
5 cloves of garlic, 4 crushed and 1 whole
1½kg (3lb 5oz) Charlotte or Desirée potatoes, peeled
500ml (18fl oz) double cream
salt and freshly ground pepper
2 tbsp freshly chopped flat-leaf parsley
2 tbsp freshly chopped chives

Lightly grease the inside of the slow cooker with butter and preheat to high.

While the slow cooker is warming, rub the whole, peeled garlic clove around the inside.

Using a mandolin or a sharp knife, slice the potatoes as thinly as possible, about 3mm (⅛in) thick. Blot the slices dry with kitchen paper.

Place two or three tablespoon-sized pieces of butter in the bottom of the slow cooker, and cover with a layer of potatoes. Overlap them slightly, if you wish. Sprinkle with crushed garlic, salt and freshly ground pepper, then cover evenly with a small amount of cream.

Repeat the layering until all the potatoes and garlic are used and the potatoes are completely submerged by the cream. Dot with any remaining butter and place the lid firmly on the slow cooker. Cook on low for 6 to 8 hours.

Garnish with fresh chives and parsley, and serve.

Options

- Stir 100g (3½oz) grated, mature Cheddar into the cream, along with one finely chopped onion, and layer accordingly.
- Crisp, lean bacon can also be layered between the potatoes, and, served with a green salad, it makes a perfect midweek meal.
- If you like your Dauphinois a little browner on top, heat a heavy-bottomed pan till it's red hot and press down on the cooked potatoes for about 3 minutes at the end of slow cooking time.

Desserts

You'll be amazed how easy it is to prepare sumptuous desserts in your slow cooker, and with the minimum of fuss. Gone are the days when slow cookers were used only for stews and casseroles; today, you can create light, moist cakes and steamed puddings, soft and flavourful fruit dishes, warm, inviting custards, and even delicious cheesecakes and crumbles. Slow-cooked desserts are not only rich and intense, but you can prepare them in the minimum of time.

Top tips for preparing desserts in a slow cooker

It is perfectly possible to bake in your slow cooker, and even packaged cake mixes work beautifully – taking all the work out of your dessert preparations. On page 131 I've included a recipe for chocolate cake using a mix, to give you an idea of how to adapt the instructions for your slow cooker. Once you've baked a cake, you can remove it from the cooker and ice it as usual, or serve it warm with a sauce. Steam or suet puddings cooked in a slow cooker are divinely moist and light, and poached fruit, fruit sauces and purées, as well as dried fruit concoctions are fragrant and sweet, while retaining the appropriate texture. A huge range of desserts work very well in your slow cooker, so go ahead and experiment. You'll need to bear the following in mind:

- For steamed puddings and some 'steam-baked' desserts, you'll need a basin, soufflé dish or tin that fits neatly into the pot of your slow cooker. Cakes and some other desserts will require a dish or tin with a lid. Alternatively, you can cover securely with greaseproof paper or foil.
- Use a lifting strap (for instructions on how to make one, see page 155) to raise and lower your basin or dish into the slow cooker.
- Most puddings and cakes will be cooked on high for the duration of cooking time.
- Fruit works best cooked on low.

- Fruits that tend to brown, such as apples or pears, should be fully immersed in liquid when cooking.
- If your slow cooker has a removable pot, you can cover desserts with crumble, pastry or meringue, and finish cooking in the oven.
- Do not exceed cooking time, as baked goods will be dry and fruit will lose its texture.
- In steam baking, dough or batter is placed inside a mould – a heat-proof and waterproof container that's placed in the slow cooker – and surrounded by about 5–8cm (2–3inches) of water. When the slow cooker is turned on, the water turns to steam that fills the pot and cooks the dough. Any heatproof container can serve as a mould, from pudding moulds to soufflé dishes to coffee cans.
- The mould should fit inside the slow cooker with space all around, to let the steam circulate properly and the dough or batter should fill no more than two-thirds of the mould.
- When you dry bake, no mould is necessary. The dough or batter can be place directly in the slow cooker. Make sure you always grease the pot carefully, to ensure easy removal. It's also a good idea to cut a circle of baking or greaseproof paper, and place it at the bottom of the slow cooker. Alternatively, look for a disposable liner, which is ideal.

Lemon Pudding Cake

This moist, zesty cake is delicious served warm or cold. A dollop of crème fraîche or mascarpone cheese and fresh mint leaves make the perfect garnish.

Serves 4–6
3 eggs, separated
2 tsp lemon zest
5 tbsp lemon juice
3 tbsp unsalted butter
375ml (13fl oz) milk
50g (1¾oz) plain flour
150g (5½oz) caster sugar
⅛ tsp salt

Beat the egg whites until stiff peaks form, then set aside. Beat the egg yolks, then blend in the lemon zest, juice, butter and milk. Combine the flour, sugar and salt and add to the egg-and-milk mixture, beating until smooth. Fold into the beaten egg whites. Spoon into the pot of your slow cooker, cover and cook on high for 2 to 3 hours.

Options
- Stir a little lemon curd into some mascarpone cheese and dollop on top for an instant 'frosting'.

Chocolate Cake

Using a cake mix might seem like a shortcut too far, but this method produces a delicious, moist cake in just a few hours. I like Betty Crocker's cake mixes, but you can use any type that serves between 8 and 12.

1 packet Betty Crocker Devil's Food cake mix
240ml (8fl oz) water
4 eggs
120ml (4fl oz) vegetable oil
100g (3½oz) dark chocolate chips

Grease the inside of the slow cooker with butter and place a circle of greaseproof paper at the bottom. Using a mixer, combine all the ingredients apart from the chocolate chips and mix on medium for 2 to 3 minutes. Stir in the chocolate chips, and tip the mixture into your slow cooker. Cook on high for 4 to 5 hours. The cake is done when a wooden skewer is inserted and comes out clean.

Options
- It's easy to make cupcakes, too! Simply prepare as above and half-fill silicone cupcake cases with the mixture. Fill the slow cooker with water until it reaches halfway up the cases and cook on high for 3 hours. A big cake has enough liquid in the ingredients to create enough steam to keep it moist and encourage it to rise, but cupcakes don't, hence the water.

Chocolate Pudding Cake

This is a rich, gooey cake that can be served directly from the slow cooker. As it bakes, it forms its own delicious chocolate sauce, making it the ultimate treat. Serve with vanilla cream or ice cream.

Serves 4–6
For the sponge
125g (4½oz) plain flour
125g (4½oz) brown sugar
50g (1¾oz) granulated sugar
3 tbsp cocoa
2 tsp baking powder
pinch of salt
120ml (4fl oz) milk
2 tbsp vegetable oil
1 tsp vanilla essence

For the sauce
170g (6oz) brown sugar
2 tbsp cocoa
425ml (14½fl oz) boiling water

Grease the slow cooker. In a large bowl, combine the first six ingredients, and mix well. Stir in the milk, oil and vanilla essence, and then pour into the prepared slow cooker. Next, in a medium bowl, stir together the second batch of brown sugar and cocoa and add the hot water. Stir until the sugar and cocoa are dissolved, then pour over the batter in the slow cooker. Cover and cook on high for 2 to 3 hours.

Options
• Stir in about 100g (3oz) chopped walnuts or hazelnuts for a nuttier flavour.

Baked Bananas with Rum and Caramel Sauce

These are a real Caribbean treat, and best served with fresh vanilla cream or ice cream.

Serves 6
6 large bananas
100g (3½oz) light brown sugar
5 tbsp salted butter, softened
120ml (4fl oz) dark rum
60ml (2fl oz) double cream
1 tsp vanilla essence

Grease the slow cooker. Don't peel the bananas, but simply make a large slit down the front of each one, from top to bottom. Mix together the sugar and butter and stuff the bananas with the mixture. Place them in the slow cooker, stuffed-side up, and pour over the rum. Cover and cook for 2 to 3 hours.

Remove the bananas, cover with foil to keep warm and pour the juices from the bottom of the slow cooker into a saucepan. Heat to almost boiling and stir until thickened. Stir in the cream and vanilla essence until combined and remove from the heat.

Place a banana on each plate and pour over the sauce.

Options
- Add 100g (3½oz) crushed walnuts to the sugar and butter mixture, then continue as above. Sultanas work well, too!
- You can sprinkle them with toasted coconut for extra crunch and flavour.

Creamy Rice Pudding with Cinnamon

This no-fuss rice pudding is creamy and delicious, and requires almost no work!

Serves 4–6
170g (6oz) pudding or short-grain rice
240ml (8fl oz) water
115g (4oz) sultanas
½ tsp salt
1 tsp vanilla extract
½ tsp ground cinnamon

Place all ingredients in the slow cooker and stir well. Cook on high for 2 to 2½ hours or on low for 5 to 5½ hours. Stir once during cooking.
    Serve warm or cold, with a sprinkling of ground cinnamon.

Options
*   For a richer cinnamon taste, place a whole cinnamon stick in the pot with the ingredients and omit the ground cinnamon.

Baked Pears

These delicious, honey-scented pears make a sophisticated dessert. Serve with a grating of dark chocolate and a little mascarpone cheese for the ultimate taste sensation.

Serves 4–6
4–6 medium pears, peeled, halved and cored
1 tbsp lemon juice
30g (1oz) toasted hazelnuts, chopped
4 tbsp runny honey
400ml (14fl oz) apple or grape juice
zest of 1 lemon

Place the pears in the slow cooker, cut-side down. Sprinkle with the lemon juice and hazelnuts. In a small saucepan, heat the honey and juice with the lemon zest until the honey has dissolved. Pour over the pears. Place the lid on the slow cooker, and cook on low for 5 to 8 hours, spooning the juices over the pears towards the end of cooking.

Remove from the slow cooker and transfer to a serving dish. Serve immediately or chill, until required.

Options
• Apples can be used in the place of pears; try adding sultanas, too.

Sticky Cinnamon Figs

These scrumptious little figs create a delicious sauce of their own while cooking. They are elegant enough to serve to guests or provide a healthy pudding for the whole family.

Serves 4
2 tbsp salted butter
8 ripe figs, with a deep cross in the top of each, and the quarters eased apart slightly
4 tbsp clear honey
handful of shelled pistachio nuts or almonds
1 tsp ground cinnamon or allspice
120ml (4fl oz) marsala wine

Place a small piece of butter in the middle of each fig, and put them in the bottom of a greased slow cooker, facing upwards. Drizzle the honey over the figs, then sprinkle with the nuts and spices. Pour the wine around the figs; it should reach about halfway up. Cover, and cook for 3 to 4 hours on low. Remove from the slow cooker, stir the juices, and pour over the figs. Serve immediately with a dollop of mascarpone cheese or Greek yoghurt.

Options
• Maple syrup can be used in the place of honey for a richer flavour.

Spicy Steamed Fruit Pudding

This is a delightfully spiced, light pudding that could easily be substituted for your annual Christmas pudding, if you are looking for something out of the ordinary. Serve warm or cold, with custard or cream.

Serves 4–6
170g (6oz) raisins
170g (6oz) sultanas
145g (5oz) self-raising flour
115g (4oz) cold, salted butter
115g (4oz) fresh brown breadcrumbs
145g (5oz) light brown sugar
115g (4oz) mixed nuts, chopped (optional)
1 tsp ground cinnamon
1 tsp ground allspice
240ml (8fl oz) milk
1 large egg

Mix all the ingredients together in a bowl and stir until combined. Tip into a greased pudding basin or soufflé dish. The pudding mixture should fill half to two-thirds of the basin. Cover with a double layer of aluminium foil, making a pleat in the centre to allow the pudding room to rise. Tie with string, then place in the slow cooker. (See page 155 for full instructions.) Pour boiling water around the basin until it reaches halfway up the sides. Cover and cook for 3 to 4 hours on high.

Options
· If you like your puddings boozy, stir 3 tbsp dark rum or brandy into the pudding ingredients.

Baked French Vanilla Custard

This rich baked custard can be eaten on its own with a spoon or served alongside your favourite puddings, tarts or cakes.

Serves 4–6
3 eggs, lightly beaten
90g (3oz) caster sugar
1 tsp vanilla essence
500ml (18fl oz) full-fat milk (or evaporated milk)
¼ tsp ground nutmeg

In a mixing bowl, combine the eggs, sugar, vanilla essence and milk and blend well. Pour into a lightly buttered pudding basin or soufflé dish which will fit in the slow cooker and sprinkle with the nutmeg.

If you have a metal rack that fits, place it in the bottom of your slow cooker. Alternatively, twist a long piece of aluminium foil and turn it into a ring, and use it instead, placing the pudding basin or soufflé dish on top. It's to prevent the dish touching the bottom of the slow cooker, which would mean the custard would cook unevenly. Add about 500ml (18fl oz) hot water. Cover the dish with aluminium foil and place on the rack in your slow cooker. Cover and cook on high for 2½ to 3 hours or until set.

Options
- Drizzle with maple syrup or dark chocolate sauce for a delicious treat.
- Berry coulis also make a lovely accompaniment to this dish.

Ricotta Amaretto Cheesecake

Ricotta cheesecakes are an Italian treat, and are lighter than the New York versions. They come in all sorts of flavours, but the toasty flavour of almond is by far my favourite.

Serves 6–8
230g (8oz) digestive biscuits, processed into crumbs
1 tbsp granulated sugar
⅛ tsp almond extract
4 tbsp salted butter
425g (15oz) ricotta cheese
230g (8oz) cream cheese
125g (4½oz) granulated sugar
3 large eggs plus 1 egg yolk
100ml (3fl oz) amaretto
2 tbsp plain flour
¼ tsp almond extract
½ tsp vanilla extract

Combine together the biscuits, sugar, almond extract and butter, and pat into the base of a springform tin that fits into your slow cooker. If it's too crumbly, add a little more butter.

Next, using an electric mixer, beat the sugar and cheeses, add the eggs and extra yolk and beat for a further 2 to 3 minutes on medium speed. Add the remaining ingredients and beat for a further 2 minutes. Pour on to the crust.

Place a rack or a ring of aluminium foil in the base of your slow cooker (see fuller instructions opposite) and put the tin on top. Cover and cook on high for 2½ to 3 hours. Turn off the heat and let it stand for a further 1 to 2 hours, until cool enough to handle. Chill in the refrigerator, before removing from the tin and serving.

Options
• Sprinkle with toasted, flaked almonds before serving.

Bread and Butter Pudding

This traditional favourite is a wonderful way to use up stale bread, and makes a comforting dessert. Serve warm with cream.

Serves 4–6
5–6 slices of bread, buttered with salted butter, and crusts removed
30g (1oz) currants
30g (1oz) sultanas
30g (1oz) dried apricots, chopped
30g (1oz) toasted almonds, sliced
2 medium eggs, lightly beaten
50g (1¾oz) caster sugar
300ml (10fl oz) milk, hot

Cut the bread and butter into small squares. Grease a soufflé dish, and place a layer of bread in the bottom of the dish. Sprinkle with the currants. Cover with a second layer of bread and sprinkle with the sultanas. Cover with the final layer of bread and sprinkle with the apricots and almonds.

Beat the eggs with the sugar, and stir in the hot milk. Continue stirring until the sugar has dissolved. Pour the mixture over the bread and fruit layers, and press down until all layers are immersed. Cover with buttered aluminium foil and lower into the slow cooker. Pour in enough boiling water around the dish to reach halfway up the sides.

Cover and cook on high for 3 to 5 hours. Serve immediately.

Options
• For a change, try using brioche or croissants instead of bread.

Blackberry Crumble

There's nothing more delicious than blackberries in season, and this delicious crumble is light, sweet and moist. You can use most fruits in season in the same way.

Serves 4–6
2 tbsp granulated sugar
2 tbsp dark brown sugar
50g (1¾oz) plain flour
½ tsp ground cinnamon
2 tbsp salted butter, melted
450g (1lb) fresh or frozen blackberries (defrosted and drained)
1 tbsp lemon juice
3 tbsp plain flour
5 tbsp granulated sugar

In a large bowl, mix together the first two sugars, flour, cinnamon and butter until combined. The mixture should be crumbly but moist enough to be pressed over your filling.

Place the blackberries, lemon juice, flour and sugar in another bowl. Stir gently to combine. Place the blackberry mixture in the bottom of the slow cooker pot and add the crumble topping. Press gently to seal the berries. Cover and cook on high for 3 to 5 hours, removing the lid of the slow cooker for the last 45 minutes or so to crisp up the topping. Your crumble is ready when the top has set, and is no longer dough-like. Serve with cream or custard.

Options
• Why not use ramekins to make individual crumbles?

Slow-cooked Fruit Compôte

This is a simple fruit dish to serve for brunch or breakfast; or serve with vanilla cream or custard for a delicious dessert.

Serves 4–6
400g (14oz) tin sliced peaches
400g (14oz) tin cherries
400g (14oz) tin sliced pears
400g (14oz) tin apricot halves
4 tbsp light brown sugar
4 tbsp orange juice
zest of 1 orange
1 tsp cinnamon

Drain fruit well. Place in the bottom of your slow cooker, then stir in the brown sugar, orange juice and zest and cinnamon. Cover and cook on low for 3 to 5 hours.

Options
- Fresh or dried fruit can be used; simply ensure that they are cut to roughly the same size to ensure even cooking, and add a little more orange juice if using dried fruit.

Chocolate Fondue

A terrific recipe for a crowd. Simply prepare the sumptuously rich fondue, lift the lid and invite your guests to dip into it with fruit, biscuits or even nuts.

Serves 6–8
450g (1lb) dark chocolate
1 tbsp salted butter
2 tbsp brandy
1 tbsp granulated sugar
300ml (10fl oz) double cream

Stir all the ingredients together in the slow cooker and cook on low for 2 to 3 hours, opening once to stir. When the chocolate has melted, whisk the mixture until smooth. Turn down the heat, leave the fondue to warm and prepare to serve.

Options
• Throw in a cinnamon stick or a teaspoon of vanilla essence towards the end of cooking time. Both will lift the flavour of the chocolate.

Sauces, Jams and Condiments

The more you use your slow cooker, the more culinary opportunities will open up for you. It can take a while to become accustomed to making the necessary adjustments to cooking times and ingredient lists, but it's well worth the effort. Everything from fresh fruit jams, zesty lemon curd, rich cheese or white sauce and chunky chutneys can be simmering away while you get on with your day.

Apricot, Orange and Almond jam

450g (1lb) dried apricots, roughly chopped
50g (1¾oz) flaked almonds
juice and zest of 3 oranges
juice and zest of 2 lemons
1kg (2¼lb) granulated sugar
2½ tsp ground cinnamon

Mix all the ingredients together and add about 1 litre (1¾ pints) boiling water. Pour into the slow cooker and leave to soak overnight. In the morning, turn the slow cooker to high and cook for 5 to 6 hours. Stir several times during cooking time, until thickened. Ladle into clean, hot jars, seal tightly and keep refrigerated for up to 3 weeks.

Options
• Add the juice and zest of 1 lime for an even zingier citrus flavour.

Crock Pot Strawberry Jam

This fresh, brightly coloured jam is easy to make, and it will last for several weeks in the fridge. If you store it in sealed jars, sterilised to manufacturer's instructions, you can keep it for months in a cupboard.

2kg (4½lb) ripe strawberries, washed and hulled
1kg (2¼lb) granulated sugar
80ml (3fl oz) lemon juice

Mix all the ingredients together in the slow cooker. Cover and cook on high for 2½ hours, stirring twice. Uncover and continue cooking for a further 2 hours, or until the jam has thickened. Stir occasionally. Ladle into hot, sterilised jars and seal, or store in the refrigerator.

Options
• Most soft fruit can be used to create scrumptious jams; raspberry and blackberry in particular work well using this recipe.

Fig and Ginger Jam

This chunky jam is warmed by the ginger, while the zesty lemon gives it a bit of bite.

1kg (2¼lb) fresh figs, stemmed, peeled and quartered
300g (10½oz) granulated sugar
120ml (4fl oz) water
1 lemon, quartered and thinly sliced (seeds removed)
2 tbsp chopped crystallised ginger

Combine all the ingredients in the slow cooker. Cover and cook on low for 2½ hours, stirring twice. Remove the lid and turn the slow cooker to high. Cook for 2 to 3 hours more, until the jam has thickened to your taste. Ladle into hot, sterilised jars and seal. The jam will keep in the refrigerator for a month or so; it can also be frozen.

Options
• Serve on toast or crumpets, or spoon over fresh plain yoghurt.

Fruity Crock Pot Chutney

This slightly spiced chutney is perfect served with sharp, mature cheeses or as a side to meat dishes.

450g (1lb) dried fruit (preferably a mixture, such as apples, peaches, mangoes, dates), coarsely chopped
450g (1lb) dried apricots, coarsely chopped
200g (7oz) raisins or sultanas
1 medium onion, peeled and chopped
150g (5½oz) dark brown sugar
500ml (18fl oz) water
270ml (9fl oz) apple cider vinegar
2 tsp Madras curry powder
¼ tsp ground ginger
⅛ tsp cayenne pepper
¼ tsp salt

Preheat the slow cooker to high. Blend together all of the ingredients and place in the hot slow cooker. Cover and cook on high for 2 hours. Turn down the heat to low, and cook for a further 90 minutes. Check periodically in the last hour or so, to be sure that it isn't overcooking. The fruit should be tender, but not lose its shape. When it's ready, ladle into hot, sterilised jars and seal. It will keep in the refrigerator for several months.

Options
- Substitute 2 tsp garam masala for the curry powder for a deeper, more fragrant taste.

Lemon Curd

Homemade lemon curd is much zestier than store-bought versions and can be used as a filling for tarts or meringues, or eaten on toast.

125g (4½oz) unsalted butter
zest and juice of 5 lemons
450g (1lb) caster sugar
4 medium eggs, beaten

Melt the butter in a saucepan and add the lemon juice, zest and sugar. Remove from the heat and stir until the sugar has dissolved. Allow to cool. Stir the eggs into the cooled lemon mixture and pour into a soufflé dish or basin. Cover tightly with foil and lower into the slow cooker. Fill the slow cooker with water until it reaches about halfway up the sides of your dish or basin. Cover and cook on low for 3 to 4 hours, until the lemon curd thickens. Stir, then pour into sterilised, warm jars and seal. Store in the refrigerator and use within three weeks.

Options
- Why not try making orange or lime curd instead?

Butterscotch Sauce

This rich, buttery sauce is the ideal accompaniment to bread and butter pudding or ice cream. You can store it in a sterilised jar and keep it for several weeks in the refrigerator.

8 tbsp unsalted butter
250g (9oz) light brown sugar
180ml (6 fl oz) double cream
pinch of salt
1 tbsp Scotch whisky
1 tbsp pure vanilla essence

Combine the butter, brown sugar, cream and salt in the slow cooker. Cover and cook on low for 1 hour. Stir in the Scotch and vanilla, whisking until well blended, and cook for another 30 minutes. Serve warm.

Options
• Omitting the Scotch will give you a more caramelly sauce, which works well with baked apples and fresh vanilla cream or ice cream.

Simple Cheese Sauce

An easy cheese sauce that can be used to accompany vegetables or pasta or layered between lasagne sheets instead of béchamel sauce.

5 tbsp salted butter
5 tbsp plain flour
salt and pepper, to taste
400g (14oz) tin evaporated milk
200g (7oz) grated mature Cheddar
2 tbsp Parmesan cheese
1 tsp mustard powder

Whisk all the ingredients together until combined. Pour into the slow cooker, cover and cook on low for 2 to 3 hours, stirring once.

Options
- Blue cheese can be used in the place of Cheddar, or, for a livelier sauce, use Red Leicester cheese with two pinches of cayenne pepper.

3 Quick Reference

Best cuts of meat for slow cooking

While any cut of meat can be slow cooked, it is the cheaper cuts (and sometimes even 'off-cuts') that tend to work best. Cheaper cuts have more connective tissue and lean muscle (as they usually come from the harder-working parts of the animal). Cooked traditionally, these cuts will be gristly and tough; in a slow cooker, the connective tissue softens and leaves the muscle beautifully soft. In fact, the gelatinised tissue remains in the meat, making it moist and tender. Cheaper cuts of meat also tend to have more fat on them, which helps both to tenderise during the slow-cooking process, and to release a rich flavour into the cooking broth. This is one reason why you rarely need to marinate while slow cooking, as the meat absorbs the flavour of the herbs, spices and cooking liquids you use.

Look out for names such as shin, leg, brisket, chuck, blade, neck, clod and skirt. All are cheaper cuts and will respond beautifully to slow cooking.

Meat	Cut	Best for
Lamb	Diced lamb (usually from the shoulder)	Stews, casseroles and curries.
Lamb	Shank	A trendy off-cut taken from the rear legs, and full of flavour. Great for any slow-cooked dish.
Lamb	Mince	Produced from trimmings of all cuts of lamb, and good for shepherd's pie, moussaka and even kebabs.
Lamb	Breast	Commonly rolled and used as a slow-cooking joint. You can also soften it up in the slow-cooker, and place it on the BBQ or grill later on to sear and impart a smokey flavour.
Beef	Casserole steak	Also known as round steak, this comes from a hind muscle. Excellent for stews and casseroles, as well as soups. Because it is lean and cooks more quickly than some cuts, it requires a little less cooking time.
Beef	Short ribs	Traditionally an American cut, these are wonderful slowly braised in wine or beer with lots of vegetables and aromatic herbs and spices.

Meat	Cut	Best for
Beef	Skirt	Usually reserved for slow cooking in either steak and kidney pudding or Cornish pasties.
Beef	Middle ribs	Boned and rolled, this is an excellent joint for pot-roasting; can also be diced for soups and casseroles.
Beef	Brisket	This comes from the belly of the animal and can sometimes be fatty; however, the fat adds to the flavour. Perfect for pot-roasting.
Beef	Diced shoulder	Not as tender as the best casserole steak, it is fine for stews and curries and particularly good for slow cooking.
Beef	Oxtail	Ideal for stews (including Osso Bucco) and soups. It's a tough cut that requires long, slow cooking, but because it is still on the bone and has plenty of fat, cartilage and marrow, it is hugely flavourful.
Beef	Shin	Lots of connective tissue here, so it must be slow-cooked to be edible. It is deliciously rich in flavour, and good for any braised dish or stew.
Beef	Olives	Made from sausage meat wrapped in thin slices of topside beef, this is

Meat	Cut	Best for
		great for stews and Mediterranean dishes.
Beef	Fillet tails	This comes from the thin end of the fillet, which is too thin for steaks or as a roast; while it is less muscular than some cuts, it creates great dishes that don't require very long periods of slow-cooking, such as stroganoffs.
Beef	Silverside	This is a neat, cylindrical joint, ideally suited to braising or pot-roasting.
Beef	Steak mince	This is created from premium cuts, and is very lean; however, it makes an excellent bolognese and moussaka, or other mince dishes that are flavourful without being too greasy.
Pork	Diced	Usually cut from the shoulder, it can also come from the gigot, which tends to be leaner. Good for stews, curries and Chinese dishes.
Pork	Mince	Meatballs, meat loaves or rissoles work well with pork mince, which has just the right amount of fat to create moist dishes cooked over longer periods of time.
Pork	Belly	This is a fatty cut, but incredibly full of flavour; ideal for casseroles and stews.

Making a pudding basin

For the perfect pud, you need to cover the basin to trap in steam, which cooks the pudding when it's placed in a saucepan of boiling water. Here's how.

Step 1: Cut a 30cm/12-in-square piece of non-stick baking paper and one of foil. Place the paper on the foil and fold in the centre to make a pleat.

Step 2: Place the foil and paper over the basin, foil-side up. Tie a double piece of kitchen string under the rim of the basin to secure.

Step 3: To make a handle, tie a double piece of string loosely over the top. This makes it easier to lift the basin in and out of the pan.

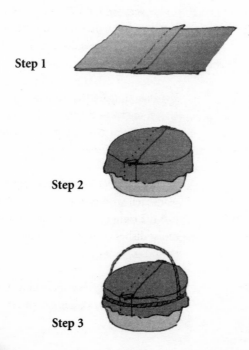

Step 1

Step 2

Step 3

Glossary of cooking terms

Beat To rapidly stir food in a circular motion. One hundred strokes by hand generally equals one minute in an electric mixer.

Blanch To drop food into boiling water for a brief period of time to preserve colour and texture or to loosen skins for peeling.

Blend To mix two or more ingredients together until combined.

Braise To brown food in fat and then slowly cook it with a small amount of liquid in a tightly covered pan. This method is best for tougher cuts of meat.

Brown To cook food quickly over high heat until the surface turns brown. This method allows the juices to stay sealed in and is usually done in a pan on your hob, or under the grill.

Caramelise The process through which natural sugars in foods become browned and flavourful while cooking. This is usually done over a constant heat of low to medium-low.

Chop To cut food into pieces ranging from small (finely chopped) to large (coarsely chopped).

Cream To mix an ingredient or combination of ingredients until soft, smooth and well-blended.

Cube To cut food into cube-shaped pieces ranging from 6mm (¼ in) to 2.5cm (1-in) long. Cubed pieces are generally larger than diced food pieces.

Cut in To work butter, lard, shortening or another fat into flour (or other dry ingredients) with your fingers, or with two knives or a pastry blender until the mixture has the texture of very course meal.

Dice To cut food into small cubes ranging from 6mm (¼ in) to 12mm (½ in).

Dust To sprinkle lightly before or after cooking with dry ingredients, such as flour, granulated or confectioner's sugar or spices.

Emulsify To bind together liquid ingredients that do not dissolve into each other. Most common is oil into vinegar or citrus juice to make a vinaigrette. The oil is poured very slowly into the acid while whisking or blending vigorously, until the mixture is thickened and the liquids become one.

Fold To gently combine a light, airy mixture (such as beaten egg whites) with a heavier mixture (such as whipping cream). The heavier mixture, placed on the bottom, is lifted from underneath with a rubber spatula and incorporated into the lighter mixture.

Fork tender Pulls apart easily with a fork (no knife required).

Pinch The amount of a dry ingredient that can be held between the tips of the thumb and forefinger. A pinch measures less than ⅛th teaspoon.

Poach To cook food in simmering liquid just below the boiling point.

Reduce To boil a liquid, uncovered, until the volume is reduced by evaporation, which thickens and intensifies the flavour.

Shred To cut, slice or tear into thin strips. Also, to pull apart very tender cooked meats, usually with a fork.

Simmer To cook liquid alone or with other ingredients over low heat. Small bubbles may appear, but liquid should not boil.

Slice To cut food into uniformly thin, flat slices. If recipes do not dictate how thinly the food should be sliced, the slices should simply be equal in size.

Soften Usually referring to vegetables, this involves heating in a pan, often with a fat such as oil or butter, and cooking, while stirring, until they lose their crunch. This brings out the natural sweetness of onions and other vegetables, such as celery.

Strain To remove solid particles from a mixture or liquid by pouring through a colander or sieve.

Zest The outer skin of citrus fruits. When grated, these are often used to flavour a wide range of dishes from main courses to desserts.

Index